Nathan Haskell Dole

The hawthorn Tree

and other Poems

Nathan Haskell Dole

The hawthorn Tree
and other Poems

ISBN/EAN: 9783743313040

Manufactured in Europe, USA, Canada, Australia, Japa

Cover: Foto ©Thomas Meinert / pixelio.de

Manufactured and distributed by brebook publishing software (www.brebook.com)

Nathan Haskell Dole

The hawthorn Tree

CONTENTS

SONGS

	Page
THE HAWTHORN TREE	3
LOVE AND MAYTIME	4
THE GRANITE CLIFF	5
THE OLD, OLD STORY	5
THE CLOSE OF A RAINY DAY	6
MY JOY	7
WILD ROSES	8
ARNE'S SONG	9
ON OGUNQUIT BEACH	10
THE BROOK	11
THE SERENADERS	13
SERENADE — I.	13
SERENADE — II.	14
SONG OF THE LONE BIRD	15
AUF WIEDERSEHEN	15

Contents

	Page
STILL MY HEART IS THINE	16
LOVE'S ASSURANCE	18
ALL THE BLOSSOMS GREET HER	19
IN MAY MY DREAM CAME TRUE	20
FERN GHOSTS	21
A FLIGHT OF HOURS	22
THE OLD STONE WALL	22
DREAM MUSIC	23
CONWAY MEADOWS	25
SUNSET	25
SPRING RAPTURE	26
SUMMER EVENING	27
SUMMER FLOWERS	28
AUTUMN IS QUEEN	28
AUTUMN MORNING	29
FORETASTE OF WINTER	30
AUTUMN SONG	30
THE LIGHTHOUSE-KEEPER	31
SONGS OF MAIZE	33

VERS DE SOCIETE

THE POVERTY PARTY	39
UNDER THE AWNING	40
LONG AGO	42

Contents

	Page
SHELLING PEAS	43
CONFESSION	46
THE BEAU OF THE TOWN	46
THE PEALING OF THE BELL	48
BLOWING BUBBLES	50
AMATEUR PHOTOGRAPHY	53
SPEAKING FEATURES	55
SCHERZO	56
MEMORIES	56
HAREBELLS	56
THE SWALLOW	57
THE BALTIMORE ORIOLE	58
MOONSHINE	59
ON THE STREET	60
A CAMEO	62
LOVE'S FIRE	63
LARKS AND NIGHTINGALES	64
TO CHLOE	65
ON RETURNING A BORROWED RING	66

SONNETS

IN THE OLD COUNTRY CHURCH	71
RUSSIA	72

Contents

	Page
SIBERIA	73
TO AN IMPERILLED TRAVELLER	74
IN THE WILDERNESS	74
SORROWS	75
MIDSUMMER NOON	76
THE TOMB OF TIME	77
QUESTIONINGS	79
ÆOLIAN HARP TONES	81
SAVONAROLA, 1498	81
ELEGY	82
THE DREAMERS	84
BEETHOVEN	85
THE STORKS	86
THE REIGN OF SATURN	87
AT MIDNIGHT'S MYSTIC HOUR	89
A PAGAN SONNET	90
EVENING	91
IN A CANOE	91
THE STORM	93
BREEZES	93
THE NETHERLAND MARTYRS, 1535	94
SPANISH SONNETS	96
PETRARCA DE SENECTUTE SUA	102
THE RIVER	103

Contents

	Page
PROPHECIES	104
HERE AND THERE	104

IN MORE SERIOUS MOOD

A RUSSIAN FANTASY	109
SUNSET FANCIES	109
THE PALACE OF PLEASURE	112
ROCKY NOOK	114
FROM A BALCONY	116
AURORA BOREALIS	117
TWO SUNSETS	117
TO A BEAUTIFUL NUN	119
PERVERTED	122
THE SHEPHERDS	122
FALLEN PETALS	126
OFF GLOUCESTER	127
GLOWING STARS	127
DISCOURAGEMENT	128
"AS YESTERDAY"	129
IN THE PARK	130
MAN'S TWO WINGS	130
IF WE WERE TO DIE TOGETHER	131
THE BROKEN VOW	131

Contents

	Page
THE HARMONY DIVINE	133
THE HEART	134
ON A PICTURE OF SUNSET IN THE ADIRONDACKS	134
PEACE	135
AT MIDNIGHT BY THE SEA	135
THE ABBÉ'S DREAM	137
THE DEATH OF AVRAHAM	138
PROPHETS	141
A LEGEND OF SAINT ANTHONY	143
AN AUTUMN FRUIT	146
THE HEROES OF CUTTYHUNK	150

Songs

THE HAWTHORN TREE

AT the edge of the hedge is a Hawthorn Tree,
And its blossoms are sweet as sweet can be,
And the bees are humming there all the day,
And these are the words that I hear them say: —
    Sweet, sweet is the Hawthorn Tree!

All the breezes that breathe o'er those blossoms rare
A burden of perfume happily bear;
And the songsters revel there all day long,
And these are the words of their merry song: —
    Sweet, sweet is the Hawthorn Tree!

And a maid and her lover wander by
As the twilight glories fade and die;
And they pause 'neath the fragrant boughs to rest,
And above them sways the robin's nest: —
    Sweet, sweet is the Hawthorn Tree!

We too, they whisper, shall soon build a home
'Neath the azure arch of the infinite dome;
And we, all the day, shall sing like the birds,
But with deeper meaning in music and words: —
    Sweet, sweet is the Hawthorn Tree!

Songs

LOVE AND MAYTIME

LOVE, gentle Love, I am weary of waiting!
　　Why hast thou lingered so long on the way?
Birds mid the boskage are wooing and mating.
　　　　　It is May!

Cold was the winter with snow-plumy pinions,
　　Holding our hearts in his insolent sway.
Now he has gone to his icy dominions.
　　　　　It is May!

Brooks down the hillsides are leaping and singing;—
　　What makes their laughter so rollicking gay?
Why are the hedges with merriment ringing?
　　　　　It is May!

Love, gentle Love, I would welcome thee gladly,
　　Yet far aloof from my roof thou dost stray.
I cannot sing, for my song would sound sadly.
　　　　　It is May!

Come, gentle Love, bring me joy without measure,
　　Make me thy debtor this jubilant day!
Here is my heart in exchange for thy treasure.
　　　　　It is May!　It is May!

Songs

THE GRANITE CLIFF

ON the granite cliff we stand,
    As the sun is sinking slow;
What a wondrous purple glow
Consecrates the sea and land!

Sails upon the changing bay,
    Trees upon the steadfast hills,
    Catch the glory as it thrills
From the arbiter of day.

As the glory fades and dies
    On the granite cliff we stand,
    Breathless, speechless, hand in hand,
Love-light kindled in our eyes.

Is our love like yonder glow
    Only for a moment's grace?
    Will it fade and leave no trace
Save the gray clouds wan and low?

THE OLD, OLD STORY

NO wind is stirring,
    There moves no leaf;
A bird forsaken
    Pours forth her grief.

Songs

The clouds hang heavy
  And darkly lower;
The rain-drops patter
  On grass and flower.

Beneath the maple
  Beyond the glade,
There come for shelter
  A youth and maid.

His arm is around her,
  He holds her hands;
And what he whispers
  The bird understands!

THE CLOSE OF A RAINY DAY

THE sky was dark and gloomy;
  We heard the sound of the rain
Dripping from eaves and tossing leaves
  And driving against the pane.

The clouds hung low o'er the ocean,
  The ocean gray and wan,
Where one lone sail before the gale
  Like a spirit was driven on.

Songs

The screaming sea-fowl hovered
    Above the boiling main,
And flapped wide wings in narrowing rings,
    Seeking for rest in vain.

The sky grew wilder and darker,
    Darker and wilder the sea,
And night with her dusky pinions
    Swept down in stormy glee.

Then lo! from the western heaven
    The veil was rent in twain,
And a flood of light and glory
    Spread over the heaving main.

It changed the wave-beat islands
    To Islands of the Blest,
And the far-off sail like a spirit
    Seemed vanishing into rest.

MY JOY

MY joy is like a sparkling stream
    That flows through flowery meadows,
Whose waters here with sunlight gleam,
And here are peaceful as a dream,
    Beneath the cooling shadows.

Songs

My joy is like a wanton stream
   Without a note of sadness,
And what care I if shallow seem
The sunny waves that dance and gleam
   And sing their songs of gladness?

WILD ROSES

O'ER the wild-rose bush
   Humming-birds hover,
Butterflies poise on the trembling leaves;
Delicate petals,
Parting, discover
Yellow-thighed honey-bees,— dainty thieves!

By the wild-rose bush
Stands a fair maiden,
Loving the flowers with rapturous eyes;
Humming-birds vanish,
Bees, honey laden,
Dart away swiftly, forsaking their prize.

Down the cool wood-path,
Where the lane closes,
Shaded by maples, rippling with song,

Songs

Comes the fair maiden,
Laden with roses —
Bright blooming roses to maidens belong!

ARNE'S SONG

BEYOND the pine-topt hills
   My eager feet would wander;
What dreams my spirit fills
   Of happy regions yonder!
I see the wingèd clouds float by;
   They sometimes rest upon the hills,
     Upon the pine-topt hills,
   And then they rise and fly
     Beyond the pine-topt hills.

Beyond the pine-topt hills
   The clouds I fain would follow.
Oh, how my bosom thrills
   To see the darting swallow!
I would delight to leave my herds
   Beneath the shadow of the hills,
     Beneath the pine-topt hills,
   And wander freely as the birds
     Beyond the pine-topt hills.

Songs

"Beyond the pine-topt hills,
  Come, brother," sing the breezes;
"For flesh obeys what spirit wills,
  And youth has what it pleases!"
"Come, brother," says the golden sun,
  And sinks behind the shadowy hills,
    Behind the pine-topt hills,
  And stars at night pass one by one
    Beyond the pine-topt hills.

ON OGUNQUIT BEACH

THE restless tide creeps up the sands;
  Like vanishing clouds the ships sail by,
In eager haste toward beckoning lands
  Across the dark blue sea they fly.
And standing on the idle shore
  We watch the sea, we watch the sky,
Changeless and changing evermore —
  We two alone, my love and I.

Our thoughts are deep, too deep for words: —
  We only with exultant eyes
Follow the ships which, like great birds,
  Will proudly sail 'neath richer skies.

Songs

We two would wander far away,
　　Where jocund summer never dies,
Where Love himself, each golden day,
　　Holds in his hand some new surprise.

THE BROOK

ALL the dreary winter long,
　　Heeding not the ice and snow,
Sang the brook his happy song,
　　Hushed and low:—
　　"Spring's advancing;
　　　Winter goes;
　　Sunbeams glancing
　　　Melt the snows.
　　Airs entrancing
　　　South wind blows;
　　Brooklet knows!"

Tinkling like a crystal bell
　　Rung by fairies underground,
With a sweet mysterious spell
　　Did it sound:—
　　"Spring returning;
　　　Joy is near;
　　Sweet is yearning;

Songs

  Dead is fear;
  Hope is burning
  All the year!
  Spring is here!"

And the willows cold and gray,
 Leaning o'er the ice-bound stream,
Heard its singing every day
  In a dream: —
  "Pussy willows,
   Sound asleep,
  Wrapt in pillows,
   Warm and deep.
  Life in billows;
   Feel it leap!
   Can you sleep?"

From the ground once brown and bare
 Forth the grass begins to look.
Soft and fragrant is the air;
  Hear the brook: —
  "Birds are singing
   Merry glees;
  Boughs are swinging,
   Mild the breeze;
  Flowers are springing
   On the leas; —
   Just see these!"

Songs

THE SERENADERS

THE night wind sleeps, the leaves are still,
    The air is rich with breath of flowers;
The moonlight creeps along the hill,—
    The waning moon of midnight hours.

We wake the night with voice of song,
    Beneath the windows of the fair;
The world is bright, and love is long,
    And youthful hearts are free of care!

SERENADE

THE hour is late, and the moon
    Hangs faint and low o'er the hill,
The great white stars in the sky
    Are shining calm and still.

The houses and the street
    Are dark and silent and lone;
But one light gleams through the night —
    My lady is watching — my own!

I lean on the wicket gate,
    And silently breathe a prayer,
That the angels of the night
    May guard the dear one there.

Songs

SERENADE

'TIS evening, and the month is June!
    Like a golden shield the moon
Hangs above the dark blue deep;
Weary winds are lulled to sleep;
Solemnly the breakers roar
On the shadowy rock-bound shore: —
    Come with me!

Above us tranquil planets shine
    With a witchery divine,
And the night's mysterious calm
Seems to pour a peaceful balm
Over all the sea and land: —
Come, my maiden, hand in hand,
    Come with me!

The languid breeze, with dewy wings,
    Sweet perfume of roses brings;
All the air is rich with flowers
Blooming in the mild night hours;
All around, below, above,
Dreams a rapturous dream of love: —
    Come with me!

Songs

SONG TO THE LONE BIRD

LONELY bird upon the tree,
   (Ah, the tree has not a leaf!)
Thou dost sing so mournfully,
   Tell me why thy grief!

Lonely bird upon the tree,
(Ah, the tree is stript and bare!)
Comes no answer back to thee
   Through the frosty air?

Lonely bird upon the tree,
(Ah, the leafless tree is dead!)
Hast thou but a memory?
   Has thy darling fled?

Lonely bird upon the tree,
(Ah, the tree will fall erelong!)
All the meaning teach to me
   Of thy plaintive song!

AUF WIEDERSEHEN

DIE Nacht enteilt; der Mond verblasst;
   Im Morgenrot' die Wolken gehen;
Die gold'ne Stund' flieht ohne Rast:—
   "Auf baldiges Wiedersehen!"

Songs

Doch muss ich scheiden, liebes Herz!
 Niemand kann seinem Loos entgehen;
Einen letzten Kuss mit süssem Schmerz
 Und dann: "Auf Wiedersehen!"

The hour is late; low hangs the moon;
 The stars are fading from the sky;
The golden night has sped too soon:—
 How can I say, "Good bye?"

Yet must I leave thee, dearest Heart!
 We may not vainly question why;
One last embrace before we part,
 And then, "Good bye, Good bye!"

STILL MY HEART IS THINE

OH, well do I remember
 How we wandered from the hill,
And followed down the lonely path
 Beside the singing rill.
At length we reached the lily pond
 Above the ruined mill,
And there upon the bank we sat
 Where all was cool and still.

Songs

The breath of lilies sweet
  Crept round our calm retreat;
The birds sang carols of love
  And in the branches above
We heard the locust shrill.
Ah! Love, 'twas love we found
  In every sight and sound,
And Love must have his will.

I know not what we whispered,
  Or if we spoke a word;
The love song of the universe
  Was sung by every bird,
And joy was echoed in our hearts
  At every note we heard.
The music of the waterfall
  The branches lightly stirred.
    The lilies so white and pure
    Told that love would endure
    And youth would ever stay:—
    It seems but yesterday—
    And years have passed away!
Yet still thine eyes meet mine,
I see the lovelight shine
As tho' it were to-day!
And still my heart is thine.

Songs

LOVE'S ASSURANCE

WHENE'ER I look into thy calm gray eyes
    Thy love smiles to me from their depths
        serene.
A heaven behind their curtain lies —
        A paradise;
  And there thy soul is seen,
        My queen!

Whene'er I hold thy shapely, firm, white hand,
  Its pressure accents what thy words impart,
Else were it hard to understand.
        In all the land
  None knows what to my heart
        Thou art!

Whene'er I walk in joyous thought alone
  Thou still art with me, walking by my side.
The silence hears the very tone
        Whereby thou'rt known
  Across an ocean wide,
        My bride.

Time cannot, distance cannot, break our bond;
  Here or hereafter thou art only mine;
If here we part we meet beyond.
        Do not despond;
  Our love in worlds divine
        Shall shine.

Songs

ALL THE BLOSSOMS GREET HER

ALL the blossoms greet her
   As she passes by;
Roses bend to meet her,
   Daisies nod and sigh: —
"She is far above us,
   No, she will not care;
Will not stoop to love us —
   Maiden pure and fair."

As she comes, the thrushes,
   Hidden in the tree,
Break the noontide hushes
   With their minstrelsy: —
"Will she deign to hear us?
   No, she will not care;
Will not venture near us —
   Maiden pure and fair."

And I wait, half hiding,
   In the bosky lane.
Shall I speak, confiding
   In a hope that's vain?
Birds have songs to sing to her,
   Flowers their perfumes bear.
What have I to bring to her —
   Maiden pure and fair?

Songs

Now she draweth nearer;
  Roses crown her brow,
All the birds sing clearer —
  They are answered now.
And her gentle greeting
  Bids me not despair;
How my heart is beating!
  Maiden pure and fair!

IN MAY MY DREAM CAME TRUE

I SAT by the brimming river;
  Blithe and early was the spring;
The waters danced and sparkled,
  And I heard the robins sing.
The south wind stirred the branches
  Of the maples plumed with green,
And the beauty of the springtime
  Filled with glory all the scene.

Along the river margin
  Came a maiden pure and fair;
The sunlight like a halo
  Touched her wayward golden hair,

Songs

The wild flowers bent to greet her
    As her footsteps kissed the grass,
The wood-birds sang their sweetest
    When they saw the maiden pass.

I sat by the brimming river
    And I watched its sunny gleams;
Blue eyes and golden tresses
    Shone responsive in my dreams.
A voice that spoke like music,
    In a tone my spirit knew,
Awoke me from my dreaming, —
    And in May my dream came true.

FERN GHOSTS

UNDER the brow of Monadnock
    These ferns came up in spring,
Curled like the crook of a shepherd
    Daintily blossoming.

Pale, now, and yellow and ghost-like
    They linger like dreams of the past,
They tell of a radiant summer
    And a love too sweet to last.

Songs

A FLIGHT OF HOURS

TO-DAY from the south came a flight of hours
   Of golden hours with welcome wings;
And where they passed grew fragrant flowers,
   And the sunbeams laughed on a thousand springs.

The gnarlèd trees on the windy hill
   Put forth a wonder of radiant white;
The meadow, yesterday bare and still,
   Was suddenly filled with the birds' delight.

And maidens forgot to be shy and cold
   When they heard the birds, when they saw the flowers,
And many a secret love was told —
   Because of a flight of sunny hours.

THE OLD STONE WALL

ACROSS the windy hill,
   And down the gentle valley
Where the wind is hushed and still,
   And pleasant waters dally,
Marked by stains of countless rains,
   Green moss and ivy clothing all,
Stretches out my grandsire's pride —
   The old stone wall.

Songs

How often when a boy,
    When summer days were sunny,
I sat in idle joy
    And ate my bread and honey.
High o'erhead the white clouds sped;
    I heard the black crows caw and call.
Ah, what a cooling shade it gave —
        The old stone wall.

And then one starry night
    The homestead I was leaving,
And life for me shone bright,
    But my sweet lass was grieving: —
"Do not weep, my troth I'll keep,"
    I said to her, "whate'er befall."
And so we kissed and parted by
        The old stone wall.

DREAM MUSIC

As one who sees a vision
    In the watches of the night,
A dream of things elysian,
    Of rapturous delight —
As one whose life ideal
    Comes forth serene and bright,

Songs

The unreal more than real
  To the quickened second sight —
Then, waking, has the yearning
  To dream the dream again,
To know the sweet returning
  Of the form recalled in vain;
So I awake from my slumbers
  With a vague unrest and pain,
For strange celestial numbers,
  For a song with a weird refrain.

It haunts me like a spirit
  From the vast halls of sleep,
By day I cannot hear it,
  Its words I cannot keep.
But oh! if I might word it
  'T would make thee smile and weep,
With smiles that thou hadst heard it,
  With tears for its pathos deep.
And when thou hearest the singing
  Of the merriest birds in May,
Or the solemn church bells ringing
  In minsters far away,
Then know that richer and sweeter
  Are the words of my roundelay,
And its harmony completer
  Than any that minstrels play.

Songs

CONWAY MEADOWS

WE sat mid the bee-haunted clover;
    The field was dancing with light;
The wind sang under and over
The bee-haunted blossoms of clover.
The wind is a wanton rover —
    His heart is free and light.

We sat mid the blossoming clover
    With the dreamy stream at our feet,
And the willows bending over,
And the lengthening mountain shadows
Came creeping across the meadows —
    Dost thou remember, Sweet?

SUNSET

THE setting sun
    O'er cloud and hill
His golden beams is flinging;
The day is done,
    The mill is still,
The robins all are singing.
    Oh, how their bosoms thrill,
And how the woods are ringing!

Songs

I sit alone,
   My window near,
Alone I sit, half dreaming;
The birds have flown,
   The stars appear,
I see the mill-pond gleaming;
   The Past is with me here,
My eyes with tears are streaming.

SPRING RAPTURE

THE air is stirred
   By winnowing wings,
And every bird
   Exulting sings;
Robin and jay
   With eager throats
Bring in the day
   With welcome notes.

Upon the sky
   Soft cloudlets sleep,
And swallows fly
   From deep to deep;
The wild geese cry
   In dizzy heights

Songs

And prophesy
    The spring's delights.

The grass grows green
    On field and hill,
And buds are seen
    With life to thrill.
When everything
    Is full of cheer
I too must sing,
    Tho' no one hear.

SUMMER EVENING

THE sky is aglow with colors untold,
    With a triumph of crimson and opal and gold,
And wavering curtains woven of fire
Are hung o'er the portals of Day's Desire.
The sun goes to rest in his western halls
And over the world the twilight falls.

The breezes sleep on the grassy pond,
And shadows rove thro' the grove beyond;
The robins carol in rapture of love,
And the martins dart thro' the splendor above.
Oh twilight marvel! mysterious hour!
Our hearts are swayed like the sea by thy power!

Songs

SUMMER FLOWERS

OH summer flowers, sweet summer flowers,
    Too soon ye fade away;
Ye cannot hold the flying hours
    That make your little day.

Oh summer flowers, fair summer flowers,
    Laugh while the skies are bright;
And sip the rich, refreshing showers
    That cool the sultry night.

Oh summer flowers, gay summer flowers,
    Be fragrant while ye may;
Sweet while ye last are woodland bowers,
    But soon ye fade away.

AUTUMN IS QUEEN

THERE is a lane behind the hill
    That leads to woodlands hushed and still.
The mossy path, o'er-trailed with vines,
Slopes gently down 'neath murmuring pines.
Its shady haunts are green with ferns,
While now the brilliant maple burns.
The asters and the goldenrod
In royal colors proudly nod.

Songs

The barberry flaunts its ruddy fire,
Red jewels swing from every brier.
Great purple grapes in clusters hang
Where late the wood-thrush sweetly sang.
The Autumn, with her wand of gold,
Will now her yearly revel hold!

AUTUMN MORNING

THE morning air is chill with rain,
    The sky is clouded o'er,
The foamy billows dash in vain
    Upon the reef-bound shore.

The ships sail on across the bay,
    Careening in the wind;
How brave and full of hope are they
    To leave the port behind!

The fisher, in his tossing boat,
    Heeds not the ocean wild;
Wrapt snugly in his tarry coat
    He dreams of wife and child.

But I sit lone upon the sands
    And watch the climbing tide;
I long to fly to distant lands,
    Across the waters wide.

Songs

FORETASTE OF WINTER

THERE'S a gleam of frost on the meadow,
   And snow on the hill beyond,
And lightly, like a shadow,
   Lies the feathery ice on the pond.

There's a chill in the breath of morning,
   A chill in the quiet of noon,
And from cold gray clouds, like a warning
   Of snow, falls the call of the loon.

AUTUMN SONG

THE leaves fall one by one,
   Though the wind is dead and still,
The gray clouds hide the sun,
   And the autumn air is chill.
        But what care you and I, my love,
           For all the changing weather?
        The darkest clouds may fly, my love,
           If we are still together.

The birds to the South have flown,
   And their songs have ceased in the land,
Silent — and bare — and lone
   The trees of the orchard stand.

Songs

  But what care you and I, sweetheart,
   And why should moods annoy us?
  The darkest days will fly, sweetheart,
   For our hearts are always joyous.

The waves along the shore
 Are breaking upon the rocks,
With melancholy roar,
 And despair as of battle shocks.
   But what care you and I, my love,
    For waves and gloomy weather?
   The darkest storms will fly, my love,
    And leave our hearts together.

THE LIGHTHOUSE-KEEPER

ON a barren isle in the midmost main,
 Where the waves chant ever their wild refrain,
Uncheered by a tree or a single flower,
Rises aloft my lonely tower.

Afar rolls the sea, till it touches the sky;
Afar the white-winged ships sail by;
They rise and fall on the restless swell,
And where they come from who can tell?

Songs

By day they mark my lonely isle
By the stately height of my granite pile;
And at night they see the friendly gleam
Of my yellow light o'er the billows stream.

Winter and summer, year on year,
Have I dwelt on this desert island drear;
My mate and I have stood by the tower,
And watched through the long nights, hour by hour.

Storms have swept from the lowering east,
The ocean has raged like a maddened beast,
Treacherous fogs have gathered around,
And deadened the alarm bell's mournful sound.

Still by the lighthouse have I staid,
And when danger pressed my heart has prayed,
Knowing full well that the Father's hand
Rules at sea and rules on the land.

But ah! when summer days have smiled
I have longed for the voice of wife and child;
But never a wife or child have I,
And a lonely man I shall live and die.

Songs

SONGS OF MAIZE

I

OH, sing of the corn —
    Of the yellow Maize,
    How it bends and sways
In the breeze of morn,
Tall and noble, with tapering spear,
Curling leaf and golden ear;
O'er the length and breadth of this bountiful land,
Beautiful gift of the Father's hand.
        Fountain of blessings, Maize, to thee!
        Sing we, bring we our lays to thee!
        Joyous and eloquent praise to thee!
        Pæans of triumph we raise to thee!
        Hail to the corn!

II

Thou wert here to welcome the Pilgrim band
    Tost by the tempest and wearied sore,
In that tiny bark by Courage manned,
    Guided by Fate to an unknown shore.
When the Winter raged in his Arctic strength
    And bowed the forests with icy blasts,
And their scanty stores were spent at length,
    And Death was the meed of their bitter fasts —

Songs

Then kernel by kernel the kind corn parched
    And burst from yellow to shell-like white,
And under the wintry sky that arched
    Like doom above them, they praised God's might.

III

Cast without care
    In rudest rows,
Wherever the share
    Thro' the clearing goes,
Tall and fair
    The bright corn grows.

Hew the trees down!
    A cabin build!
Skies smile or frown,
    Thy land is tilled,
And the mould rich and brown
    With the Maize is filled!

IV

Skies grow gray;
Short the day;
With the sickle reap away!
    Reap the corn;

Songs

Bind in sheaves
Ears and leaves;
Rich the harvest man receives;
It is Plenty's overflowing horn!

Ripe and dry,
Pile it high,
Now the creaking wain goes by
To the barn!
Fields once fair
Now are bare,
Only stubble lingers there!

On the floor,
More and more,
Bustling with the rustling store,
Lay the corn!
Splendid gain!
Golden grain
Flowing from the loaded wain;
It is Plenty's overflowing horn!

v

Hither! merry men and maids!
Come at even, young and single!
Eyes will sparkle, cheeks will tingle,

Songs

'T is the Autumn Husking-bee!
    Give your aid!
    Who 's afraid,
If a purple ear one see?

Jocund speech and racy song,
    Ripples of light silvery laughter
    Circling round the dusty rafter;
    Who would ask
    Brighter task
Than to husk with such a throng?

Follows now the country dance;
    Strike up, Jerry, with your fiddle!
    Swiftly up and down the middle
    Gayly skip,
    Smile on lip,
Youth and maid, retreat, advance!

Then along the dusky lane,
    Minding not the nipping weather,
    Shy young couples stroll together.
    Love confest,
    Love is blest
With the husking of the grain!

Vers de Société

THE POVERTY PARTY

AUTUMN it was and the evenings were long;
    Sure it was time for a wee bit of fun;
Music and dancin' can never be wrong
When the day's labor is over and done.
Twenty-four couple we gathered in all
At the Poverty Party at Papineau's Hall.

All of us poor folk, but all of us young,
High beat our hearts with the joy of full life;
None of us lads but was secretly stung—
Stung with the hope of possessin' a wife.
Never again will such pleasure befall
At a young people's party at Papineau's Hall.

Cornet and organ made music divine;
Smooth was the floor and bright the lamps gleamed;
Brighter than stars did Peggy's eyes shine;
She was the lassie of whom my heart dreamed,
She was the gayest, the belle of the ball,
At the Poverty Party at Papineau's Hall.

Waltzes and schottishes, polkas and reels,
Followed each other like gems on a crown;
Peggy paid heed to my fervent appeals,

Vers de Societe

Ten times or more I wrote her name down.
And I took her to supper and carried her shawl,
At the Poverty Party at Papineau's Hall.

Late was the hour when the party was done,
Yet the last dance would none of us miss;
Seein' 'em home was the cream of the fun.
Peggy — she gave me her first little kiss.
Now we are old, but we often recall
The Poverty Party at Papineau's Hall.

UNDER THE AWNING

'TWAS a summer evening, cool and charming;
    Every seat upon the Common held its blissful twain;
Boomed the beetles by them quite alarming,
  And the foliage rustled like the dropping of the rain.

Perfumes from the buds of roses rising
  Woke ecstatic raptures from the rose lips of the fair.
That soft hands were claspt is not surprising,
  Nor that waists were clipt and kisses stolen unaware.

Vers de Société

I too sat with Mary 'neath the awning,
   While the sickle moon with Venus gemmed the
      golden West;
And I felt the tender passion dawning,
   Like a moonrise o'er the heaving ocean of my
      breast.

"Dearest Mary, wilt thou be my star, pet?
   Yes, I vow, 'tis thou alone on earth whom I
      adore!
When we're married, Mary, not a carpet
   Need we have upon our lovely inlaid wooden
      floor!"

Ah! how confidentially we whispered,
   Cheek to cheek, while melancholy toads chirped in
      the trees,
And our mothers not the slightest lisp heard
   As they sat within the parlor, talking charities.

Many years are garnered since we planned it,
   That our house should have no carpet on the inlaid
      floor.
Gentle reader, canst thou understand it?
   I was six then, and my neighbor, Mary, she was
      four.

Vers de Societe

LONG AGO

I REMEMBER the grove near the village
  Which the brook ran murmuring through,
And the shady retreat by the still edge
  Of the pond where the willows grew.
In springtime, in summer, I went there —
  I wonder if any one knew
Of the many long hours that I spent there,
  First with Mary, and then, Maud, with you!

The flowers that grew on the hillside
  Seemed fragrant as those of Cathay,
The breeze o'er the bright daffodils sighed —
  Or were they but buttercups gay?
The pond the lily-pads covered,
  The lilies gleamed white in the sun,
And above them the dragon-fly hovered,
  Like the flash of a scintillant pun.

Ah, Maud, how the birds used to sing there,
  In the trees that kissed overhead!
Kissed? *We* never did any such thing there —
  "'T was too improper," you said.
But I brought you gay flowers by the lapful,
  And wove graceful crowns for your hair,
While you filled the band of my cap full,
  And gave me a garden to wear.

Vers de Societe

Oft we sat on the slope (eating sorrel!)
    While the wind in the pine branches sobbed,
And the mischievous squirrel would quarrel
    With the robin whose nest he had robbed.
But we thought not of quarrels in those years,
    Nor heeded the sighs of the pine,
Any more than the chubs mid the osiers
    Ever dreamed of the fish-hook and line!

SHELLING PEAS

(A Summer Idyl.)

AT the back door of the kitchen,
    Sitting on the foot-worn sill,
Looking toward the pine woods which in
    Beauty crowned the westward hill,
Thrilling 'neath the necromancy
    Of the south wind in the trees,
Sat together Nick and Nancy,
    Eager rivals, shelling peas.

On the chestnut tree a squirrel
    Chuckled o'er his stolen nut,
While two robins saw some peril
    (They could not have told you what)

Vers de Societe

In the actions of a kitten
    Chasing her elusive tail: —
Other rustic sights, unwritten,
    Charmed them as they stormed the pail.

Now, while Nancy's peas still held out,
    Nick had reached his very last,
And with all his panful shelled out
    From his lap the dish he cast,
Scaring off the careless neighbor's
    Chickens from the strawberry bed,
Startling Grandma at her labors
    With the butter in the shed.

Then Nick took from blushing Nancy
    Half the peas as yet unshelled
(He could in the polished pan see
    Pouting sweet rebellion quelled!)
And together fingers nimble
    Quickly finished up the work.
"Look," cried Nick, "here is a symbol!
    In this pod predictions lurk."

So he broke the smallest pea-pod:
    It contained two little peas.
"See, my Nancy, we may reap odd
    Stalks of truth from things like these!

Vers de Societe

These two peas are you and I, dear,
   Dwelling in one pod of bliss,
Cool it looks and green, inside here;
   Would you like a home like this?"

Round the slender waist of Nancy
   Nick's insinuating sleeve
With a thrill of joy, I fancy,
   Stole, and waited not for leave.
And upon her lips he printed
   (In large type) a fervent kiss,
While a sob from Nancy hinted
   Her deep ecstasy of bliss.

*   *   *   *   *   *   *

Hark! the cockerel from the Jones's
   Barnyard sings his loudest lay,
And the Bantam cock intones his
   Wishes for "the happy day."
And the half-oblivious couple
   Heed not jibe of beast or bird,
Or the father coming up hill—
   Is not "Young Love" too absurd?

Vers de Societe

CONFESSION

IT was a charming day, my dear,
    An August day some years ago;
From me you ran away, my dear,
    Down thro' the shaded walk you know.
I saw your fluttering drapery
    White mid the sun-fleckt trees like snow.
I followed to the grapery
    And there I found you all aglow.

And when I kissed your cheek, my dear,
    To pay you for the way you sped,
You pursed your lips to speak, my dear;
    Do you remember what you said?
You said, "I love"—ah! yes, you did,
    Why then, I pray, this tell-tale red?
You said, "I love"—confess you did!—
    "'I love sweet grapes' was what I said."

THE BEAU OF THE TOWN

HE once was young and gay,—
    A beau.
But that was long ago;
    To-day
He is very old and gray.

Vers de Société

His clothes were once the best;
      His tile
Was at the top of style;
      His vest
Was flowered upon his breast.

He then was tall and slim;
      His eye
Made all the maidens sigh
      For him.
It now is bleared and dim.

He drove a handsome pair
      Of grays,
And all men sang his praise;
      The "heir"
Had plenty and to spare.

He now is poor and lame
      And bent;
His sunshine friends all went,
      And shame
To take their places came.

The flowers upon his vest
      Are rags;
His coat is torn and sags.
      The rest
May easily be guessed.

Vers de Societe

His youth was spent in vain;
    His age
Is like a blotted page;
    His bane
Was sparkling bright champagne.

THE PEALING OF THE BELL

MY little lady went one day
    A-sailing in a yacht
Upon the waters of the bay —
    'T was summer time and hot.

The wind at first had promised well,
    And filled the spinnaker;
But ere they reached the Point it fell:
    The craft seemed not to stir.

The skipper stood beside the wheel,
    And cocked his weather eye,
And wet his thumb if he might feel
    A zephyr wandering by.

And while they drifted with the tide
    A mile or so from shore,
My little lady multiplied
    Her stock of naval lore.

Vers de Société

She learned the different kinds of rig
    That on the deep are seen —
"Hermorphodite" and sloop and brig,
    Schooner and barkentine.

She learned the terms that so confuse
    A maiden country bred:
That "sheets" on ships they do not use
    To make a sailor's bed.

That "come in stays" means merely "tack,"
    That booms are said to "jibe" —
And many more which from the lack
    Of space I can't describe.

And when a breeze sprang up at last,
    And gently 'gan to sough,
She gazed at bowsprit and at mast,
    And cried, "She springs her luff!"

The skipper let her take the wheel,
    And steer the bonny craft;
How proud the pilot fair did feel!
    How merrily she laughed!

Now "starboard" and now "hard-a-port"
    The wheel was swiftly turned.
(Yes, steering was her special forte,
    I since have surely learned!)

Vers de Societe

The breeze it blew, the blue waves danced,
    The graceful yacht careened,
And still the burning sunbeams glanced
    From brow and nose unscreened.

What wonder that when morning came
    (The cruise a past delight!)
My fair one's face was all aflame,
    Her dainty nose a sight!

But when the cuticle came off
    (Her nose was *retroussé*),
I felt inclined to laugh and scoff,
    As fondest lovers may.

"My dear," said I, "you know full well
    What sore distress I feel,
And yet 't is proper that a belle
    Like you should sometimes peal."

BLOWING BUBBLES

AH! how far away and dreamy
    Are the summers of my youth;
Ere I knew that life was seamy,
    Ere I learned the bitter truth.

Vers de Societe

Golden-colored, free from troubles
    Were those days of long ago —
But they vanished like the bubbles
    That we children loved to blow.

Often to the mossy house-top,
    High among the swaying elms,
(Where no moment did the boughs stop
    Fencing as for airy realms),

Would we bring our bowl of water
    And our fragile pipes of clay —
I and our next neighbor's daughter
    (She is dead now) — little May.

All around us rival thrushes
    Revelled in the lists of song,
And the locust in noon hushes
    Shrilled his trumpet loud and long.

Far above us swept the swallows
    In swift races through the sky,
Mid the cloud-land hills and hollows,
    Playing hide-and-seek on high.

Far below us lay the river
    With its placid azure gleam,
Where the sunbeams all a-quiver
    Scarce disturbed its peaceful dream.

Vers de Societe

Every rock and tree and dwelling,
    And the orchard, row by row,
On the hillside upward swelling,
    Had its counterpart below.

We could see the shadows racing
    With the sunshine, frown with smile,
Where the lindens interlacing
    Made a Gothic minster aisle.

And the quaint unpainted steeple
    Of the church that faced the green
Seemed to watch the buried people
    Like the guardian of the scene.

On the house-top sat we gayly
    Blowing bubbles, unconcerned,
As like vessels fashioned frailly
    Off they sailed and ne'er returned.

Breezes swept them in derision
    On their brief and brilliant flight;
Then they vanished from our vision
    Like young hopes of dear delight.

Still I see that scene before me,
    And the fine old country-seat,
And remembrance rushes o'er me,
    With its bitter and its sweet.

Vers de Société

> Radiant hours of childish pleasures
>   Catch the sunlight as ye will,
> Youth and age have different measures,
>   But our joys are bubbles still.

AMATEUR PHOTOGRAPHY

I FELL in love with Phyllis Browne;
  She was the nicest girl in town.
Her father had a bank account
Of a superfluous amount;
And so the more I thought of it
The clearer seemed the benefit
That such a union would confer
At least on me — perhaps on her.
For she was pretty! Such a nose!
Such grace of curves! Such tint of rose!
Such sylph-like elegance of pose!
Such sunny eyes of heavenly blue,
With little cherubs peeping through!
Such golden bangs! Oh, every such
Was the superlative of much!

And educated! She could speak
Italian, Spanish, Volapük,

Vers de Société

French, Russian, Swedish, Danish, Dutch,
Choctaw and Sanskrit, Latin, Greek;
And every language born of Babel
To read or speak them she was able.
So learned, pretty,— rich besides,
Yes, she would be the gem of brides!
And I, tho' poor, had every taste
The wealth of Crœsus would have graced;
So I resolved to risk my fate
In winning such an equal mate.

At first my chances promised fair;
She met me half-way everywhere;
Accepted my civilities,
And sometimes made me ill at ease
When I, on parting, held her hand,
And felt that mute "You understand,"
Exprest by just the faintest squeeze.
(I can not think she was a flirt,
And yet she did it to my hurt!)

One day I crost the Rubicon
And went to win my paragon.
I rang her door-bell, inly bent
On knowing if she would consent.
She sent me down a little note,
The coolest that she ever wrote.

Vers de Société

"Excuse me, please, from seeing you,
I've something else that I must do;
I'll see you later if we live."
I asked the footman if he knew
Why such an answer she should give.
The servant shrewdly shook his head;
"She's busy, sir," he gravely said,
"Developing a negative."

SPEAKING FEATURES

WHENEVER I talk with my sweetheart
    She speaks with her great brown eyes;
And if (and 't is often) I'm witty,
    A gladdening smile replies.

If (rarely) I grow sentimental,
    And out-Romeo Hamlet the Dane,
With a golden-lined cloud on her forehead
    She frowns me to wisdom again.

And if I sing her some love song,
    And show all the feeling I can,
The rose on her cheek is her "Thank you":—
    Oh, I am a fortunate man!

Vers de Societe

SCHERZO

WOULD I keep the "I" from sight?
　　Ay, I would blind it.
For when self I lose aright,
　　Then alone I find it.

MEMORIES

A FADED flower will touch the key
　　Of many a sacred memory:
A yellowed note, a crumpled glove,
Will call up visions of young love,
And make the heart beat fast again
At sweet remembrance mixt with pain.

HAREBELLS

HOW wild the steep along the hill
　　Where rocks grow bold and bolder!
There harebells grow in fond alliance
With pine trees looking down like giants,
　　And every little crevice fill
　　With purple bells that yet are still
While nodding sweet defiance
　　To every chance beholder.

Vers de Société

THE SWALLOW

Of all the birds that swim the air
    I'd rather be the swallow;
And, summer days, when days were fair,
    I'd follow, follow, follow
The hurrying clouds across the sky,
And with the singing winds I'd fly.

My eager wings should need no rest
    If I were but a swallow;
I'd scale the highest mountain crest
    And sound the deepest hollow;
No forest could my pathway hide,
No ocean plain should be too wide.

I'd find the sources of the Nile,
    I'd seek the Liukiu Islands,
Climb Chimborazo's snow-capt pile,
    And Scotland's rugged Highlands;
I'd skim the sands of Timbuctoo;
Constantinople's mosques I'd view.

I'd revel mid the Isles of Greece —
    The pride of old Apollo,
And circle round the bay of Nice,
    If I were but a swallow.
And haunt the sunny fields of France —
The vineyards merry with the dance.

Vers de Societe

I'd see my shadow in the Rhine
    Dart swiftly like an arrow,
And catch the breath of eglantine
    Along the braes of Yarrow;
I'd roam the world and never tire
If I might have my heart's desire.

THE BALTIMORE ORIOLE

ON the elm branch gayly swinging
    Where the tender young leaves curl,
Sits a Golden Robin singing:—
  "Pretty girl,
    Pretty, pretty, pretty girl."

All day on the branch above me
  While the purple leaves unfurl,
He is asking: "Dost thou love me,
  Pretty girl,
    Pretty, pretty, pretty girl?"

Then he hears his brown mate's answer
  From the hedge that skirts the lane:
"Catch me, catch me, if you can, sir,
  I can fly, though I am plain."

Vers de Société

But he cares not as he swings there
    Mid the springtime's rush and whirl;
Still he blithely clings and sings there,
    "Pretty girl,
        Pretty, pretty, pretty girl."

MOONSHINE

THE red moon hangs on the sky
    Like the shield of a viking bold,
And across the ocean waves
    Lies a track of molten gold.

It leads to the sea-king's realm,
    Beyond our eager sight,
And there is his palace of pearl
    And his throne of diamond bright.

His chariot, dolphin-drawn,
    And his Tritons with puffed cheeks,
Have never come to our shores
    Since the days of the gallant Greeks.

By the crest of the weed-fringed reefs
    No Naiads comb their hair,
Nor now do the Sirens sing
    So treacherously fair.

Vers de Societe

But follow that path of light
   Beyond the tumbling main,
And there will the mermaids dance
   And the Sirens sing again.

ON THE STREET

AS I walked the street,
   Melancholy, lonely,
Came the vision sweet
   For a moment only.

Not a star was out,
   Tho' the day was ended;
Darkness as of doubt
   From the clouds descended.

All my work had failed,
   I was worn and weary;
Skies of joy were veiled,
   Night fell black and dreary.

Not a soul I knew
   In the mansions splendid;
Tithes of bitter rue
   In my heart were blended.

Vers de Societe

Then I caught the gleam
   Of a heavenly vision,
Brighter than a dream,
   Of a scene elysian.

'T was a homelike room,
   Rich and warm and cosy;
Thro' the evening gloom
   Streamed the firelight rosy.

Children sat around,
   Gladness on their faces;
There, thought I, abound
   All the Christian graces.

Then a maiden fair
   Came to draw the curtain.
Breathless stood I there,
   Trembling and uncertain.

With her hand upraised
   And her pure face lifted,
Spirit-like she gazed
   Thro' the darkness rifted.

Then the curtain fell:
   But that scene of gladness
Worked a magic spell
   On my cloudy sadness.

Vers de Société

Framed in rosy light,
    Still that unknown maiden
Beams upon my sight,
    When with grief I'm laden.

As I walked the street,
    Melancholy, lonely,
Came the vision sweet
    For a moment only.

A CAMEO

QUEEN PENELOPE all the day,
    Weaves a robe of glistening white;
    "It is almost done," her suitors say,
"Soon shall we feast on the wedding night."
But in silent hours as her tears fall fast,
    She ravels the woof, she begins anew;
And thus fly the years until at last
    Odysseus comes, her hero true.

A garment of snow Dame Nature weaves,
And when at night her spirit grieves
Her tears melt the woven snow away;
She begins again on another day.
The north winds cold are the suitors bold
But Summer comes ere the year grows old.

Vers de Societe

LOVE'S FIRE

WHAT a glowing fire
    Young Love kindles
With the fuel
Of desire!
When 't is fairly started
  How he tends it!
When it dwindles
  How at first he mends it!

Is he tender hearted?
Nay, he's cruel:
  For at last
  When the novelty is past,
Weary grown
  Of the dying embers,
  He no more remembers
That the fire was once his own.

Lets the flashes
Fade in ashes
  Gray and cold!
  Young Love soon grows old —
      And that ends it.

Vers de Societe

LARKS AND NIGHTINGALES

ALONE I sit at eventide;
    The twilight glory pales,
And o'er the meadows far and wide
Chant pensive bobolinks.
(One might say nightingales!)

Song-sparrows warble on the tree,
I hear the purling brook,
And from the old "manse o'er the lea"
Flies slow the cawing crow.
(In England 't were a rook!)

The last faint golden beams of day
Still glow on cottage panes
And on their lingering homeward way
Walk weary laboring men.
(Oh would that we had swains!)

From farmyards, down fair rural glades
Come sounds of tinkling bells,
And songs of merry brown milkmaids,
Sweeter than oriole's.
(Yes, thank you — Philomel's!)

Vers de Societe

I could sit here till morning came,
All thro' the night hours dark,
Until I saw the sun's bright flame
And heard the chickadee.
(Alas! we have no lark!)

We have no leas, no larks, no rooks,
No swains, no nightingales,
No singing milkmaids (save in books) —
The poet does his best.
It is the rhyme that fails!

TO CHLOE

SEE! I have returned thy picture
   As thou didst request.
But I hold another, better,
  In my breast.

If I would, I can not send it;
  It will not depart.
'Twas thyself who didst engrave it
  On my heart.

Vers de Société

ON RETURNING A BORROWED RING

IF, while the world lay wrapped in sleep,
   And midnight stars begemmed the sky,
From some far cavern dark and deep,
   Where delve and toil the Genii,
My potent will could hither bring
   A giant ready to obey,
By reason of my lady's ring
   And the strange magic of its sway: —
What should be then my swift commands?
   What errands should he haste to run?
What should he bring from Orient lands,
   Or trackless realms beyond the sun?

Ah! he should bring me sparkling gems
   In golden caskets chaste and rare,
And brilliants set in diadems
   To glitter in my lady's hair.
And every morning in her room
   A jar of roses he should set,
Awaiting but her smile to bloom
   With fragrant crystal dewdrops wet.
All should be lavished at her feet
   Without her knowing whence they came,
And in her joy my love would meet
   A recompense without a name.

Vers de Societe

But vain are wishes; rings are vain;
   No talisman wakes magic powers,
And idle fancies bring but pain
   To lonely hearts in weary hours.
So I my lady's ring restore: —
   'T is but a band of yellow gold
Through which I see the world and more —
   So much the circlet small can hold!
And if to me the Genie came,
   I were his slave (as I am thine!) —
How could I dare to breathe thy name
   E'en should my longing lips incline?

Sonnets

IN THE OLD COUNTRY CHURCH

IS it a dream?   Am I once more a child?
   In this old church I worshipped long ago!
   Again I feel the strange, delightful glow
That filled my young heart with a radiance mild,
While from the organ-loft the tones, beguiled
   By skilful hands, harmoniously flow,
   Now swelling high, now welling faint and low,
As tho' harsh discords all were reconciled!

Outside, the graceful elm boughs softly sway;
   Thro' the open windows breathes the summer
      breeze;
And in the hush before the people pray
   I hear the murmur of a myriad bees.
Is it a dream?   Am I a child to-day?
   It verily seems so, as I bow my knees!

Ah! golden hours of childhood gone forever!
   My brown-eyed, quiet little maiden there
   Who feels but knows not what is meant by prayer
The time must come when she too will endeavor
Her weary heart from sad to-days to sever,

Sonnets

To lift the burden of a present care;
Then will she to the Father's house repair
To find sure comfort.   May it fail her never!

The summer breeze will sweep the cloudless sky;
  The yellow bees will hum among the elms;
The mellow organ tones will swell and sigh;
  The priest will speak his words of counsel sweet
To guide the wandering soul to heavenly realms:
  And thus each age its marvels doth repeat.

RUSSIA

"Russia! Russia! I behold thee from my wondrous beautiful distance." — GOGOL.

SATURNIAN mother! why dost thou devour
  Thy offspring, who by loving thee are curst?
Why must they fear thee who would fain be first
To add new glories to thy matchless dower?
Why must they flee before thy cruel power,
  That punishes their best as treason's worst —
  The treason that despotic chains would burst —
That makes men heroes who in slavery cower?

Upon thy brow the stars of empire burn;
  Thy bearing has a majesty sublime.
Thy exiled children ever toward thee yearn;

Sonnets

Nor should their ardent love be deemed a crime.
O, mighty mother of men, to mildness turn,
  And haste the advent of a happier time!

SIBERIA

"ALL hope forego, O ye who enter here!"
  Here winds are sweet with breath of myriad flowers,
The skies arch blue o'er lands of richest dowers,
And all the fairest gifts of earth appear.
All hope forego? Why, surely hope, not fear,
  Should view this land, whose belting Ural towers
  With wealth of gold and precious stones, and powers
Of mighty rivers winding far and near!

Yet look! What mean those melancholy trains
  Of desperate men and sad-eyed women, looking back
    To bid that awful bourne a last farewell?
O hear those groans, those sighs, those clanking chains,
  As on they drag along the hopeless track
    That leads, if not to death, to worse than hell!

Sonnets

TO AN IMPERILLED TRAVELLER

UNFLINCHING Dante of a later day,
    Thou who hast wandered thro' the realms of pain
    And seen with aching breast and whirling brain
    Woes which thou wert unable to allay,
What frightful visions hast thou brought away:
    Of torments, passions, agonies, struggles vain
    To break the prison walls, to rend the chain—
Of hopeless hearts too desperate to pray!

Men are the devils of that pitiless hell!
    Men guard the labyrinth of that ninefold curse!
    Marvel of marvels! Thou hast lived to tell,
In prose more sorrowful than Dante's verse,
    Of pangs more grievous, sufferings more fell,
    Than Dante or his master dared rehearse!

IN THE WILDERNESS

AS one who, wandering thro' some tropic land,
    Content with all the tropic's languorous ease,
    Amid the tangled maze of giant trees
Chances on ruined temples, vast and grand,

Sonnets

On broken sculpture hurled on every hand,—
   The fallen column and the crumbling frieze,—
   By man abandoned countless centuries,
And marvels and can only silent stand,—

So I, rejoicing in thy sunny heart,
   Loving the danger of thy radiant eyes,
Have heedless strayed into a realm apart,
Deep hidden in thy life,— a ruined realm
Of joys and hopes which years with death o'erwhelm,—
   And sorrow fills me with a dumb surprise.

SORROWS

THE clouds which fleecy are and silver-lined,
   As high above us joyfully they fly,
   And seem like living creatures in the sky,
Sporting and racing with the free, glad wind,
When near us are but mists, damp and unkind,
   Which gloom the azure heaven, and coldly lie
   Upon the hills and fill the valleys. Ay,
Thus sorrows are within the human mind.

For other's woes are tinted with romance;
   We watch them from afar and feel them not,
Excepting as they shade the sun by chance,

Sonnets

And add new zest to our delightful lot.
But let them on us like a storm advance,
How swiftly then our gladness do they blot!

MIDSUMMER NOON

I

BENEATH the noontide sun the valleys lie,
  Swooning with heat and full of golden light;
The swift-winged swallows cease their busy flight,
Slow shadows across the dreamy landscape fly,
As fleecy clouds drift o'er the azure sky.
  The robins sing no longer in the trees;
  From the wild alder floats the hum of bees;
A locust shrills upon the elm near by.

The sweet-toned bell up in the square church tower
  Breaks on the silence, and the wooded hills
Repeat the sound, which of the resting hour
  To mowers laboring in the hay-fields tells;
Hanging upon some low-limbed tree the scythe,
To lunch they hasten, weary and yet blithe.

II

Beneath the shadow of an old oak tree,
  My friend and I lie on the velvet grass:
  Amid the leaves the whispering breezes pass,
And the small crickets chirp incessantly.

Sonnets

The distant, cloud-like mountains we can see,
   Heaped on the west in deep diaphanous mass;
   And at our feet — a living sea of glass —
The pond is sleeping in tranquillity.

Silent we are. The calmness of the scene,
   The quiet beauty of the summer day,
   Says more than any words that we can say.
Silence means more to us than speech can mean.
'T is joy enough against the oak to lean,
   And dream the perfect hours of peace away.

THE TOMB OF TIME

I

IT was the midnight hour. I stood alone
   Beneath the stars in a deserted land,
   Where cold winds swept across the wastes of sand,
Amongst the meagre herbage making moan.
I saw a pyramid of polished stone,
   Black as the blackest ebony, and grand
   As though it had been built by God's own hand;
A gloomy temple Death might call his own.

A portal was upon the northern side,
   And fiery letters in an unknown tongue;

Sonnets

And from the arch a flaming censer hung,
Which threw a baleful radiance far and wide.
   I saw the massive gates were open flung,—
I wished to enter, but my courage died.

II

And as I pondered trembling, lo! there came
   Across the yellow sands a solemn throng;
   The air was burdened with a mournful song,
And torches, flaming with a ghostly flame,
Weird shadows cast upon an ebon frame,
   Whereon a coffin lay with trappings hung.
   With slow and solemn tread they moved along,
And reached the portal of the mystic name.

They entered and I followed. With a clang
   The gates shut to, and thro' the vaulted hall
The awful echoes, thundering, rang and rang,
   And died away in tones funereal.
   Then on my ear did saddening music fall,
And tear-choked voices with an organ sang.

III

A dirge they sang unto the year just dead,—
   The old year which had reached the Tomb of Time.
   I heard the organ and the voices chime,
But not a dead year lifted up his head.

Sonnets

Silent they lay as when they first were laid,
  With all their records of good deeds or crime,
  In niches fated by a Fate sublime;
For Fate by even Time must be obeyed.

I saw them lying there, all cold and still
Each in his place,— dead years, the vanished past.
  I saw the places kept for coming years
  Where crownless they should lie beside their peers.
And lo! I saw there was one less to fill,
For in his place the Old Year lay at last.

QUESTIONINGS

THE PESSIMISTIC ANNIHILATIONIST

FETTERED to earth and powerless to fly,
  I envy those white clouds with wide-stretched wings,
  Who, scornful of us earth-born, grovelling things,
Exult in all the freedom of the sky.
For what of liberty have such as I?
  What is the comfort aspiration brings,
  And what the glory that the poet sings?
What can man do but lay him down and die?

Sonnets

On all sides are we closely hedged about.
   We know not such a boon as liberty.
   Fools we! to dream of ever being free.
Our highest aspirations end in doubt.
   Our so-called glory is a mockery;
And Death itself is but a blotting out.

THE PANTHEIST

What! Death a blotting out? Yes, thou art right;
   But so the stars are blotted out at morn,
   When in the east the joyous Day is born,
And from her presence flees the gloomy Night.
The stars are lost in more effulgent light.
   And what is life on earth but night forlorn?
   So when the day of death comes, Night is shorn
Of its small glory by Day's greater might.

Dost thou not think that over all is One —
   A God, who rules amid the seeming rout,
Who curves the steadfast circle of the sun,
   And whirls the myriad flaming worlds about?
Canst thou, then, think thy life forever done,
   Because at death thy candle seems put out?

Sonnets

ÆOLIAN HARP TONES

"solvitur acris hyemps grata vice veris et favoni."

THE south wind thro' my open window blows.
    It trembles into music on the strings
Of an Æolian harp, and sweetly sings
A quaint and mystic song, which louder grows,
Then dies away, until so soft it flows,
    We hardly hear it.   And the voice is Spring's!
    She to the waiting Northland comes!   She brings
The modest Mayflower and the fragile rose!

E'en now the birds among the trees are flying,
    And now the willows clothe themselves in green,
    And many a crocus in the field is seen.
Far off unseen we hear the wild goose crying,
    The world is filled with Spring's own smile serene;
For thus she greets us, swiftly hither hieing!

SAVONAROLA, 1498

AS on some noble mountain height I stand
    And see the promise of a golden day,
    While still the vales below are cold and gray,
And night hangs brooding o'er a sleeping land.

Sonnets

I, conscious of the glory near at hand,
  With burning eyes of faith, exultant, stay
  To catch the first glimpse of the godlike ray
Ere down the mount it leaps in progress grand.

Awake, ye dormant nations, now awake!
  Behold the sun of Truth is risen on high!
Out from the bonds of superstition break,
  And claim the splendid prize of liberty!
Forget the dead past for the future's sake;
  Where falls the broken tree, there let it lie!

ELEGY

I

THE air is full of mournful melodies,
  As if the birds had left a song behind —
A requiem which the melancholy wind,
Transforming to Æolian harmonies,
Repeats in whispers to the sobbing trees.
  Hark to the elegy of unwept tears —
  Of struggling hopes and of despairing fears —
A poem played in tender minor keys.

The summer days are gone — the birds are fled.
  Upon the field and hill the grass is brown,
  The yellow leaves come fluttering softly down,

Sonnets

And rustle on the path beneath the tread.
    The glories which were once the Summer's crown
Are vanished, and the Summer now lies dead!

II

The trees were royal in their autumn gold —
    Their robes were rich with orange and with red,
    Their banners proudly to the winds were spread,
And to the Frost-king waved defiance bold.
Yet now no more their boasted power they hold.
    Their little day of royalty was sped,
    Their little gleam of glory quickly fled,
As passed the kingdoms of the kings of old.

With leaden clouds the sky is dark and gray;
    The rain falls on the faded, yellow leaves.
    With bitter teardrops saddened Nature grieves —
She weeps because her beauty fades away.
Is this the future which the buds of May
    Gave promise of?   Ah, smiling Spring deceives!

III

Yet as the day is drawing to its close,
    And as the Sun sinks in the arms of Night —
    Among the clouds appear great rifts of light,
And all the gray is glorified with rose,

Sonnets

The hue of hope, which fainter, fainter, grows,
   Until at last it vanishes from sight.
   Then on the yellow sky, divinely bright,
The sickle moon above the horizon glows.

How soon forgot the sadness of the day!
   Night hides beneath the shadow of her wings
The presence of the demon of decay,
   And throws her mantle over dying things;
The spirit of life and love stirs in our clay,
   For we behold Night's star-dust in endless rings
And only see the stars — Night's coronet!

THE DREAMERS

SOME men are dreamers born; their mystic souls
   In visions never realized are wrapt.
  They for the life around them are inapt,
Like hermits idly reading mystic scrolls.
Where angel heads glow with their aureoles,
   Or strange lands are mysteriously mapt
   With mighty streams and mountains thundercapt,
Or where the organ fugue silently rolls.

Sonnets

Alas, these dreamers! How the world goes by them,
  With all its living joys and living sorrows.
  And as they watch for never-coming morrows,
They lose what ought to bless and sanctify them.
  For while the Future dazzling promise borrows,
The wasted golden Present lingers nigh them.

BEETHOVEN

I

WHERE art thou now, O master, where art thou?
  Is thy soul busied with the harmonies
Which God hides in those rolling stars of his,
Silent to us — to thee apparent now?
Where art thou now, O master, where art thou?
  The world has missed thee long, and none there is
  To be, like thee, the Priest of Mysteries,
And wear the diadem upon the brow.

And yet the world is full of thee. Thy name
  Is synonym for highest in thine art,
And brighter thro' the coming years shall shine.
Would I might add a little wreath of mine —
  Alas, how insignificant a part —
To place within the temple of thy fame.

Sonnets

II

I love the ocean's glorious symphonies
  In nature's everlasting solitudes;
  The deep adagio of its peaceful moods;
Its light allegro when the white caps rise;
Its minor when the sunset zephyr dies;
  Its mighty major when the storm cloud broods
  And sweeps the straining harp-strings of the woc
And far on high the foaming water flies!

So when Beethoven's magic music swells,
Like voices of the angels heard in sleep,
  My spirit to its utmost depths is stirred
  As though a more majestic sea I heard,
As though some sunken city's silver bells
Swung palpitating in the purple deep.

THE STORKS

AT midnight, when the sleeping world is still,
    And bright-eyed stars, like watchmen, gu
        the sky,
  And look down calmly from their posts on high
O'er field and forest, ocean, stream, and hill,—

Sonnets

From ruined tower and long-deserted mill
   Uprise the friendly, wide-winged storks, and fly
   Straight to the sunny lands which southward lie,
Beyond man's ken, beyond all thought of ill.

Man would not harm them: they are sacred things.
   Their scarlet bills and scarlet legs are known
   From Nile to Ganges; and from Rhine to Rhone
Is heard the flapping of their dusky wings.
They are affection's symbol; for, Love sings,
   The mother stork will perish for her own.

THE REIGN OF SATURN

*" aurea prima sata est aetas qua vindice nullo
sponte sua, sine lege, fidem rectumque colebat."*

THE legend says that in the golden time
   When Saturn's sceptre blest the blooming earth,
Men's hearts were filled with overflowing mirth,
And love and peace dwelt in that happy clime.
For never yet had thought of war or crime
   In simple guileless bosoms had its birth,
   And never yet had cruel, wasting Dearth
Dared enter where reigned Plenty in her prime.

Sonnets

Men lived as brothers, and their lives were long;
   Their lives were free from discord, free from care.
All day the woodlands echoed to the song;
   And sounds of feasting filled the evening air.
And often came the glorious gods among
   These happy men, their sweet delights to share.

*"postquam Saturno tenebrosa in Tartara misso
sub Jove mundus erat."*

But Jove against his father Saturn rose,
   And harshly drove him from his ancient throne.
   Then wandered forth the crownless god alone,
His hoary head bent low with weight of woes,
Leaving his kingdom to his sons,— his foes.
   Sad was it for the world when he was gone.
   Peace from the mourning earth, and joy were flown.
War on the heels of Hatred followed close,
And Famine spread her black wings o'er the land.
   O then, those miserable men were fain
   To have their father Saturn come again;
Were fain to have the feet of Plenty stand
In her old Temple; and dread Famine bound.
   Alas! alas! their wishes were in vain.

Sonnets

AT MIDNIGHT'S MYSTIC HOUR

I

AT midnight's mystic hour I climbed the hill
    Whose farther slope dips gently to the shore.
Like a vast prayer the solemn ocean's roar
Rose ceaseless from the rocks; all else was still —
So still that I could hear the young grass thrill
    As from the whispering night air, warm once more,
    It won the impulse from the ground to soar —
As if, poor rooted thing, it might at will!

A few great stars begemmed the tender sky,
    And, like the swords of serried Seraphim
        Drawn up for battle far away from earth,
The Northern Lights flamed to the zenith high
    And swept in triumph to the horizon's rim,
        While in the east a meteor died in birth.

II

I flung myself upon the dewy ground
    And fixt mine eyes upon the mighty maze
    Of twinkling constellations, and the blaze
Of flaming swords that crossed without a sound —
So far, so weird, so changeful, in profound

Sonnets

Obedience to the unknown Power that sways
　The universe, and that the planets praise
As swift they circle in their endless round.

There as I prostrate lay and strove to scan
　The scope of those fierce forces bound to law,
　And felt the joy of inexpressible awe
At such a divine weft of rhythmic plan,
　A tiny night moth fluttering by I saw
And wondered if God had less care for man.

A PAGAN SONNET

THE silent mountains, purple robed, like kings,
　　Stand waiting for the coming of the night.
They feel her solemn presence as the light
Fades slowly from their crowns. The sun-god flings
His last red beams, tingeing the silver wings
　Of clouds rejoicing in their eastward flight.
　Will they be first to see his chariot bright
Emerging from the ocean, when he brings
His bride, the Day, to glad the world again?
　Ah! soon they vanish from our yearning sight,
In darkness flying on, their fate the wind.
The rosy hues of hope are fond and vain.
　Fate is relentless; love is quenched in night.
Farewell, ye clouds, to your own future blind!

Sonnets

EVENING

THE crimson glow has faded from the west;
   Deep shadows lie along the glassy stream,
In whose cool depths green banks and daisies dream
Of green banks and of daisies which are blest
With real existence and with perfect rest,
   While they themselves are not, but only seem.
   The katydids pipe up their cheerful theme;
The bird is sleeping in her woven nest,
And near her sighs the melancholy breeze.
The fire-flies, like lost, wandering Pleiades,
With intermittent light dart through the trees.
The evening stars smile down with radiant eyes,
And fiery swords wave on the northern skies,
As if to guard the Aurora's Paradise.

IN A CANOE

I

DOWN in the sea caves sinks the dying sun,
   The restless waves are tinged with Tyrian hue,
   And purple clouds are hung upon the blue
Of heaven, until the heaven and sea are one.
Where ends the sea? Where is the sky begun?
   I, floating in an Indian canoe,
   With all these glories round me, with the view

Sonnets

Expanding as the waves I ride upon
Lift up their haughty heads, could I not sail,
   Until I reached the line where sea and sky
   Are blended into one infinity?
Could I not float out on the sea of space,
   And learn new wonders from behind the veil
Which hides from us God's everlasting face?

II

The day fades and the solemn, mystic night
   Broods with her thousand stars upon the ocean;
   The winds are hushed,— calmed is the waves' commotion;
The crescent moon pours out her jar of light
Upon the waters. Clouds as silvery white
   As angels' wings, float with the softest motion
   Across the sky and pay their deep devotion
Unto their queen, enthroned on heaven's height.

O Sea — thou symbol of almighty power!
   O Night — thou majesty of majesties!
My soul is humbled at this solemn hour,
   Surrounded by thine awful mysteries.
May my vain yearning slowly die away
As dim Night took the sceptre from the Day.

Sonnets

THE STORM

FROM some far valley of the West arise
    The storm clouds like the hordes of Tamerlane,
And marching on in awful silence gain
The zenith-posted fortress of the skies.
The courier wind on wingèd courser flies
    And brings the pelting volleys of the rain.
    And then the loud-voiced thunder bursts amain
And echoes on the circling hills, and dies.

The mighty hosts of Nature cannot spare.
    They hasten on to work their destined death —
        Across the summer seas the darkness sweeps,
    The white-sailed boats go down before its breath;
        From heaven the jagged lightning blindly leaps
Nor heeds the agony of human prayer.

BREEZES

SOME people meet us like the mountain air,
    And thrill our souls with freshness and delight;
    And others are like cooling winds of night
To fan the heated brow of busy care;

Sonnets

And some are like the summer breezes, rare
  With perfumes, breathing from the gardens bright
  Where flowers are blooming, far beyond our sight.
And so we know the gardens must be fair.

And such we welcome when the day is done,
  And gentle melancholy seasons mirth,
When fading tints across the gray sky run,
  And darker shadows brood upon the earth.
  Then deep heart confidences have their birth,
And holy, life-long friendships are begun.

THE NETHERLAND MARTYRS, 1535

I

AMID the flames their souls were full of cheer,
  And, facing the dark mystery of death,
Unflinchingly they clung unto their faith,
No whit relenting at the beck of fear.
And while the crowd stood round to mock and jeer,
  These martyrs blest them with their dying breath,
  Remembering what the Holy Scripture saith:—
For they were noble men although austere.

Sonnets

They died — unhonored for their constancy.
   Brave men were they; yet no one mourned or
      wept.
They suffered for the sake of liberty;
   And in their death, their deathless fame is kept.
   But had they lived, their story would have slept
Uncared for in the tomb of history.

II

The faith they held was bigoted and blind.
   The God they worshipped was a cruel God.
     A rugged and a weary path they trod;
And life's delights they, murmuring not, resigned.
So when the summons came to leave behind
   Life's bitterness, they bowed beneath the rod,
   And gladly laid aside the fettering clod —
A martyr's never-fading crown to find.

Their names are lost to us, but their example
   Flames like a beacon thro' the mist of ages,
And bids us bravely stand when men would trample
   Upon our faith, and overthrow our altars;
When fiery persecution round us rages,
   And when our courage under trial falters.

Sonnets

SPANISH SONNETS

I

FOR many a day my heart no song has sung,
    For many a day my lips no music made;
The harp which oft of old my fingers played
Is silent, with its silver strings unstrung.

Ah, wearily the sad days drag along,
    With never a ray of joy their gloom to cheer;
    Alone I sit and mingle sigh with tear;
Alone I sit and nurse my fancied wrong.

But mayhap she, the cause of all my woe,
    Is grieving that her lover comes not near,
    Is sadly wondering why she doth not hear
The low notes of his dulcet serenade
    Beneath her window ere the sweet stars fade —
Come, heart of mine, I pray thee let us go.

II

Beneath my lady's window soft I crept;
    The music of far waters lulled the night;
    On high the queen moon walked in garments bright,
And up the east lordly Orion swept.
Beneath my lady's window watch I kept,

Sonnets

And let the slow hours wing their silent flight,
   The while I envied e'en the moonbeams white
That kissed my spotless lady while she slept.

The rosy flush of morn was swiftly stealing
   Across the mountains as I turned away,
And lo, I saw her by her casement kneeling,
   With palms together prest to greet the day;
And matin-bells across the fields came pealing,
   And all the world in glittering sunlight lay.

III

I hied me home and sang my songs once more;
   I took my dusty harp and tuned it well,
   And when I touched its strings, there came a spell
Upon me such as song-birds feel that soar
High toward the sun and all their heart outpour
   In sweet, melodious strains, which rise and swell,
   And to the world their rapturous joyance tell.
So played I as I ne'er had played before.

For though I had but seen her from afar,
   Yet did my heart know that she prayed for me.
For mystic soul-communings oft there are,
   More faithful than mere human speech can be.
And ere I saw her, from the pole a star
   Fell, like God's benediction, silently.

Sonnets

IV

The golden moments fly like yellow bees,
    Which come with honey from the daisied field,
    The golden moments all their sweetness yield,
Their flowery sweetness, honeyed memories.
Ah! memories, too sweet for perfect peace,
    Unless I share them; yet my lips are sealed.
    Would not the charm be lost if I revealed
That name, to me so full of harmonies?

No hour, no moment, in the livelong day,
    But is weighed down with honeyed thoughts of thee.
Imprinted on the night's page, dim and gray,
    Thy smiling face, thine eyes, thy form, I see.
The music of the ocean far away,
    Without thy name in it, discord would be.

V

I wonder if none wonder why I smile,
    As thinking of my love I walk the street,
    And see not, neither hear the folk I greet,
But only see my one love all the while.

Sonnets

I traverse many a long and joyous mile
   Of fragrant groves, whose checkered branches meet;
   They know, they tell me of my maiden sweet;
My heart with songs of her the birds beguile.

'T was only yesterday I saw my love,
   'T was only yestermorn I saw my own,
   Beside her open casement sitting lone,
With eyes fixt on the mountain heights above.
She saw me not, and I gazed from afar,
As one who worships the pale evening star.

VI

The deepest, cruelest love is love unspoken,
   Which battles with itself — passion with passion;
   White fire with lurid fire — in such fierce fashion
That love's self dies, and lo! the heart is broken.
And yet the steadfast spirit gives no token,
   Tho' red-rose cheeks may pale, tho' lips grow ashen;
   Like thin-faced monks who lash without compassion
Their quivering limbs to punish sins unspoken.

   Keep silence, oh, my heart! be thou no traitor;
Betray not thy wild struggles, thy wild yearning.
   Yea, let thy agony seethe as in a crater

Sonnets

Hidden by flowering vines far down is burning
The lava seen but by the All-discerning.
   Great is thy love, fond heart — my will is greater.

VII

Maybe in God's own time, when time is past,
   Love incomplete shall be made full and round
   By perfect joining of lost parts, and crowned
By the rich jewel of God's love at last.
But why should we endeavor to forecast
   The problem of the future?   Life is bound
   With adamantine chains.   We hear no sound
From those who vanish in death's awful vast.

Were it not best, then, once, only once, to speak —
   To kiss; then part as if the past were not?
Life has no deeper vengeance on men's hearts to wreak.
   Nay, silent suffering is a nobler lot.
I will be strong because I am so weak;
Though I should die for Love's sake — for Love's sake.

VIII

How the fresh raindrop on the grass-blade flashes!
   Behold the sunbeams on the river dancing!
   See the swift swallows thro' the deep sky glancing!

Sonnets

Hark, how the fountain in the arbor flashes!
How Nature mocks us as we sit in ashes!
   I thought she wept with me — now is she lancing
   Her bitter shafts of sunshine down, enhancing
My griefs! O Nature, how thy joyance clashes!

Yet why? The dimmest star-heart sympathizes
   With our distress; and mayhap through our sorrows
Our poor love purer, higher, nobler rises.
Love on in silence, then, O heart! and grieve not,
   For after sad to-days come happier morrows.
That love is lost believe not — oh, believe not!

IX

The sun sinks down behind the purple hills
   And delicate clouds in golden radiance glow;
   The splendor brightens o'er the sea below,
And all the conscious world with beauty thrills.
The sea is calm; the sighing south wind stills,
   The ripples on the beach scarce come and go,
   As slowly up the sands the waters flow
And the full tide the crescent harbor fills.

Alone I sit upon the rocks, alone
   And watch the light upon the headland far —
   It kindles like the silvery evening star.

Sonnets

The phantom ships sail on and fade away
As night broods o'er the silence of the bay;
And still I sit and think of thee, my own.

PETRARCA DE SENECTUTE SUA: A PARAPHRASE

quas humilis tenero stylus olim effudit in aevo
perlegis hic lachrymas, et quod pharetratus acuta
ille puer puero fecit mihi cuspide volnus.
omnia paulatim consumit longior aetas,
vivendoque simul morimur, rapimurque manendo.
ipse mihi collatus enim non ille videbor;
frons alia est, moresque alii, nova mentis imago,
voxque aliud sonat:
pectore nunc gelido calidos miseremur amantes
iamque arsisse pudet. Veteres tranquilla tumultus
mens horret, relegensque alium putat ista locutum.

The tears which in my callow youth I shed
   Long since are dried; the wound made by the dart
   Of Love, the archer, on my boyish heart
Is healed. The summer of my life is dead,
And one by one its idle joys are fled.
   Like Death, our daily living bids us part
   From all we once held dear. O Time, thou art
Our Fate, which drives us with relentless tread!

Sonnets

The old self that we knew is now no more.
   The brow is wan; fond habits suffer change;
   The mind has other eyes; the voice is strange.
Our cold hearts pity lovers passionate;
   We blush that once we burned. Old loves we hate;
And former vows we deem another swore.

THE RIVER

THE river is a moody human thing;
   It laughs whenever the sky is sunny blue,
While from the sky it takes a richer hue.
Nothing it does all day but laugh and sing,
And toss its diamonds like a wayward king.
   And if the day is dark and sad, then too
   The river mourns the hours of sadness through,
And seems dissolved in tears of murmuring.

It is a sympathetic, soulless soul —
   A creature touched by every passing breath,
   For future sunshine it has little faith —
Remembers not the past. Now is its whole.
Though it knows not, it rushes to its goal —
   Its goal the mighty ocean's living death.

Sonnets

PROPHECIES

Sweet is the homage which the south winds show —
  Sweet is the piney incense which they bring
  To delicate, proud harebells, as they swing
Their graceful heads, a-nodding to and fro.
The organ tones o' the sombre pines is low —
  Low the prophetic hymn their branches sing.
  Is it a sound of the ocean murmuring?
Does it reach the river in its ceaseless flow?

Beneath the brooding banks the waters stay;
  Entranced, they listen to the oracle
  Which of the sea the sun-fleckt pines foretell —
Singing the doom to which they haste away.
Thus mortals, hurrying to Eternity,
Catch sometimes a faint sound of its vast sea.

HERE AND THERE

The sunshine slants across wide fields of green,
  The wind drives bending billows o'er the grass
  Chased by the shadows of white clouds that pass
Like kindly dragons down the blue serene.

Sonnets

Afar the dreamy mountains hedge the scene,
  Ethereal in their opaline transparent mass:
  Not with my naked eye nor with my glass
Can I redeem the miles that lie between.

If on yon cloudlike mountains I should stand,
  The land would lie as though upon my palm —
  The rivers — silver ribbons, the blue lakes calm
Like mirrors echoing sunny gleams of skies;
And far away my village, like a band
Of little pearls, where this fair valley lies.

In More Serious Mood

A RUSSIAN FANTASY

O'ER the yellow crocus on the lawn
  Floats a light white butterfly.
Breezes waft it! See, 't is gone!
  Dushka, little soul, when didst thou die?

SUNSET FANCIES

WHERE glows the sunset
    Like a fiery ocean
  Do you see the islands,
      The Hesperides?
Green are their palm trees,
    Somnolent in motion,
      Musical in silence,
          Bending in the breeze.

Many are the herds there
    On the meadows straying—
      Snowy-fleeced sheep,
          Wide-hornèd kine.
Many are the red deer
    On the hillsides playing;
      See how they leap!
          How their antlers shine!

In More Serious Mood

See, in the tree-tops
    Splendid birds are flashing,
        Living gleams of color,
            Living tongues of flame!
See the lofty fountains
    Musically plashing —
        Diamonds are duller,
            Every drop's a gem!

Shaded by palm groves,
    Halls of alabaster
        Strangely carved with stories
            Of departed days,
Sculptured by chisel
    Of no earthly master,
        Glow with golden glories,
            With precious stones ablaze.

They are the mansions
    Of the old Immortals,
        Exiles from earth
            Long centuries ago.
Amaranthine wreaths
    Crown their pearly portals;
        Never-dying mirth
            Is theirs, never thought of woe.

In More Serious Mood

There Ganymede,
    For the gods reclining
        On golden couches,
            Bears the jewelled bowl;
There the ancient poets,
    In white raiment shining,
        With rhythmical touches
            Wake the harp's deep soul.

There is Athene
    Standing by her altars,
        Grave and sublime,
            Watching o'er her fane.
Faith in her godhead
    Never wanes or falters;
        She in good time
            Will be worshipped again.

There is the Temple
    Of the good Apollo,
        Where light like wine
            Spouts in living jets.
Round the vast rotunda
    Scarce the eye can follow
        To the heights divine
            Of starrèd minarets.

In More Serious Mood

Out in the ocean
    Of the sunset glowing
        Have you seen this vision —
            Those Islands of the Blest?
Have you seen the temples,
    Seen the fountains flowing,
        And the hills Elysian
            In the purple west?

Now darkness gathers;
    Night with sable pinions
        Forever shuts away
            That glimpse of Paradise.
Jealously guarding
    Her infinite dominions,
        Keeping from day
            The secrets of the skies.

THE PALACE OF PLEASURE

WE have read in legends of old
    Of palaces built in a night;
With walls of glittering gold,
    And roofs of crystalline light;
With stores of treasures untold,
    Collected from deep and from height.

In More Serious Mood

At sunset the site is a waste
  Of tangled, unfructified ground,
By fens and quagmires defaced,
  Where reptiles and serpents abound:—
A paradise spoiled and debased;
  No rose sheds its fragrance around.

At midnight assemble the powers:—
  The gnomes and the djinns from the earth,
The fairies that lurk in the flowers,
  The Titans that forge works of worth,
The weavers of magical bowers,
  To build the beautiful birth.

In silent and cheerful array,
  In orderly cohort and line,
The workers their master obey,
  By his will, without signal or sign,
The wizard exhibits the way,
  As tho' by a wisdom divine.

The briers and brambles are banned,
  The marsh is transformed to a lake,
Tall trees on the avenues stand,
  Clear fountains in rivulets break.
A new paradise blooms in the land
  Ere the birds in the morning awake.

In More Serious Mood

Foundations of marble are laid;
   Like visions arise the fair walls;
Silken tapestries now are displayed;
   Long mirrors show jewel-set halls;
The chambers, richly arrayed,
   Are thronged with obedient thralls.

And thus when the magical car
   Brings home the prince and his bride,
All things in readiness are
   To welcome their lord and their pride.
And music swells, echoing far,
   And banners and pennants float wide.

The Palace of Pleasure is done.
   In a night it is built. In the day
It will vie with the light of the sun.
   In an hour it may vanish away.
So joy like a cobweb is spun.
   The prince and his bride — where are they?

ROCKY NOOK

THROUGH his breezy bower of leaves
   Gleams the golden oriole,
Pouring out his joyous soul
As his hanging nest he weaves.

In More Serious Mood

In the sunny fields the quail,
   Hiding deep mid nodding flowers,
   Whistles for the coming showers —
Cheerful tho' his omens fail.

O'er the meadow hovering,
   Near the winding brooklet's brink,
   Trills the lyric bobolink —
Our Anakreon on the wing.

See! upon the topmost leaf
   Of the maple on the hill
   He is swinging, singing still,
Like a soul that knows no grief.

How the air with perfume swoons!
   Humming dart the yellow bees
   From the flower-clad apple trees;
All their lives are honeymoons.

Insects chirp amid the grass,
   Swallows twitter as they fly
   Arrowlike across the sky,
And the crows call as they pass.

Thro' the night the whippoorwill
   Threatens from the linden tree,
   And the voices of the sea
All the solemn silence fill.

In More Serious Mood

Silvery music from the brook,
  Rapturous singing from the field.
  Golden moments dost thou yield,
To thy lovers, Rocky Nook.

FROM A BALCONY

I SEE a patch of woodland,
  A hill which hovels crown,
A wide brook overflowing
  With waters dull and brown.

Then black lines of a railway
  With swift trains thundering by;
Like comets manned by demons
  In headlong speed they fly.

Below me is a courtyard,
  Unshaded by a tree;
A mournful bush in the corner
  Is its only shrubbery.

And there a withered leaflet
  Spins round in the fitful wind,
Like a sad gray ghost imprisoned,
  No exit can it find.

In More Serious Mood

The type of many a mortal,
  That wan leaf has no rest,
And I think that a grave in the churchyard
  For you and me were best.

AURORA BOREALIS

IN the cold midwinter night,
    O'er the frosty northern sky
Gather spectral armies bright.
See them march and wheel and fight —
    Fight and fall and die!

So the mystic hosts of thought
    Thro' my soul at midnight gleam;
Valiant battles then are fought,
Doughty deeds are swiftly wrought.
    Is it all a dream?

TWO SUNSETS

ONCE before I saw a sunset
    From this rocky hill,
Saw the valley deep and misty,
Saw the mountains blue and still,
And the crimson clouds above them
    With the sunbeams thrill.

In More Serious Mood

But 't was not so much the sunset
   Which ensouled the place,
As it was the glow and glory
Beaming from thy raptured face,
Wistfully, unconscious of me,
   Gazing into space.

Now once more I see the sunset
   (Years have had their flight),
See the misty valley darkling,
See the mountain's purple light,
And the dusky-shadowed pinions
   Of the eagle, Night.

But alone I see the glory!
   Dearest, thou art far!
And the clouds grow black and heavy
Shutting out the evening star,
And my heart is sad and weary,
   Crushed by Fate's stern bar.

Though I know that day returneth,
   And the night is gain,
Yet I cannot lift the burden
Of the present's grief and pain.
Darkness closes in around me —
   Courage, trust, are vain.

In More Serious Mood

TO A BEAUTIFUL NUN

FAIR Nun, that slowly wanderest
    Thro' byways of the town,
Tell me the thoughts thou ponderest,
    Demure, with eyes cast down.

The world around is beautiful;
    No joy to thee it brings,
Because thy spirit dutiful
    Is set on heavenly things.

The sunlight is not vanity,
    Nor pleasure sign of ill;
Bright greetings of urbanity
    May tender heartstrings thrill.

But all these things are naught to thee;
    Such visions thou must shun.
Another code is taught to thee,
    Thou solemn-vestured Nun.

Thy talents,— make no use of them
    To win the world's applause;
Such use were but abuse of them
    To hurt Religion's cause.

In More Serious Mood

Thy voice, tho' rich and glorious,
    Must not in mirth take part;
Thy hands must be laborious
    In charity, not art.

Thy face would grace society,
    Thy hand be sought in love;
But all thy realm is piety;
    Thy heart is fixt above.

Yet calm and unregretfully
    Thou goest on thy way,
As tho' desire were met, fully,
    In that one word "obey."

No thought of earthly joy disturbs,
    For earthly love must cease;
No trivial annoy disturbs
    The current of thy peace.

Surrounded by thy purity
    As by an angel's arm,
Thou passest in security
    Amid all sin and harm.

Sweet bride of heaven, abidingly
    Thy thoughts all heavenward flow;
And thus alone, confidingly,
    Thou walkest here below.

In More Serious Mood

The sombre garb thou wearest here,
    The rosary, the cross,—
Symbol of what thou bearest here,—
    Make all things seem but dross.

Above, the wedding raiment waits,
    The crown, the promised spouse;
For all the loss the payment waits,
    The answer to thy vows.

For this thou hast forsaken all
    Thy beauty might have won;
For this alone hast taken all
    The sorrows of a Nun.

Fair Nun, my heart acknowledges
    A pang to see thy face.
I care not for theologies,
    I only care for grace.

And yet I would not change thy lot
    To that of mortal bride.
Let God alone arrange thy lot
    And in thy heart abide.

In More Serious Mood

PERVERTED

A LITTLE, innocent, white-winged Cloud
    Flew out across the summer sea,
And there was met by a surly crowd
    Of Fogs and Tempests. She tried to flee.

"Now join us," cried a menacing form,
    "Or else thy beauty we destroy!"
When back she came with the hosts of storm
    Destruction was her only joy.

THE SHEPHERDS

I

SHEPHERDS, have ye heard the story?
    Shepherds, did ye see the light?
All the sky was filled with glory;
    Hill and vale were bright.

II

Shepherds, we our flocks were keeping
    On the upland pasture ground;
All the world around was sleeping;
    There was not a sound!

In More Serious Mood

III

As we stood alone and listened
   To the silence near and far,
Suddenly before us glistened,
   In the East, a star.

IV

Brighter in its swift ascension
   Than the planet or the moon,
Soon it claimed our rapt attention:
   Night was turned to noon.

V

In affright we drew together,
   All we shepherds on the hill,
And our wonder questioned whether
   It should bode us ill.

VI

When it came and hung suspended,
   Blazing over Bethlehem:
Every rock, with radiance splendid,
   Sparkled like a gem!

In More Serious Mood

VII

When we found ourselves surrounded
   With a bright angelic throng,
And above us, round us, sounded
   Loud a wondrous song.

VIII

Harps of gold and crowns undying,
   Robes of white and jewelled wings!
On our faces we are lying
   While the seraph sings:

IX

"Peace on earth! Good will to mortals!
   Christ the Lord this day is born;
He hath passed the heavenly portals,
   Glorious is this morn!

X

"Blessed tiding to all nations!
   God hath sent to ransom them.
Go and find him! Loud ovations
   Sing in Bethlehem!"

In More Serious Mood

XI

Then the mighty angel chorus
  Clove the air with sweet acclaim;
Swelled the hymn, resounding o'er us,
  Hailing Jesus' name!

XII

Shepherds, we have straightway started,
  Leaving on the fields our sheep,
To discover, joyful-hearted,
  Where the Babe doth sleep.

XIII

Seek with us the blessed Stranger!
  Come adore the heavenly Child
Lying in the humble manger,
  Pure and undefiled!

XIV

Angels, wondering, hover o'er him;
  Costly gifts the Magi bring;
And the rabbis bow before him,
  Mutely worshipping.

In More Serious Mood

XV

And his gentle virgin mother
  Holds him closely to her breast:
On the earth there is no other
  Woman half so blest.

XVI

Shepherds, now you know the story
  Of this wondrous Christmas morn.
Let us also share the glory
  Of the King new born.

FALLEN PETALS

ON the ground — on the dewy ground —
  Lie the apple blossoms strewn around.

Yesterday — only yesterday —
All the boughs with fragrant blooms were gay.

But a wind — a dark wind — arose,
And they fell — drifting like the snows.

So thy heart, with hope's petals strewn,
Misses now the blossoms thou hast known.

Never fear! The fruit will load the tree,
And Life's autumn bring some good to thee.

In More Serious Mood

OFF GLOUCESTER

UPON the lifting curve of the sea
    The fishing fleet drifts dreamily,
And the sky looks down with its tenderest smile;
And the ocean, forgetting his craft awhile,
Takes the ships on his heaving breast
And brings them into the port of rest.

GLOWING STARS

TELL me, glowing stars on high,
    Do I perish when I die?
Or shall I be ever I?

Will my spirit have re-birth
And regain the things of worth
When my dust returns to earth?

Ye too perish, ye too fall:
Flash a moment — then the pall:
Is that typical of all?

Boundless depths of glowing spheres,
Changeless in the changing years,
Seem to negative our fears.

In More Serious Mood

Yet your changeless is all change!
Fleeting, flying on, ye range
Thro' the vortex vast and strange.

Other creatures, other men,
Cling upon you, live — and then
Do they die and live again?

DISCOURAGEMENT

SAID the glowworm: "I,
A creature of fire,
Cannot touch my desire;
However I yearn and try
To meet and greet
My winged sisters high
In the sky —
I can only burn and die!"

Said the firefly: "I,
A creature of light,
Cannot wing my flight
Thro' the luring night
To my calmer sisters high
In the sky!

In More Serious Mood

I can only fly
Over field and flower
For my little hour,
And die like a sigh."

Said my fervent soul:
"I'm a creature of light and fire;
But why — why should I aspire?
For ne'er may I rise higher
Than the glowing coal
On the funeral pyre,
And Death is my goal!"

"AS YESTERDAY"

A SWEET young mother fell asleep and died:
   She left her children to a stranger's care;
Yet scarcely had she reached the other side
   When all her dear ones gathered round her there.

A Spirit saw the wonder on her face: —
   "They lived on earth their rounded lives," it cried,
"But Heaven knows naught of measured time or
    space: —
   A hundred years have vanished since you died!"

In More Serious Mood

IN THE PARK

THE dry leaves rustle on the ground
    With weird, mysterious, whispering sound.
What is the secret that they tell?
"We are hapless ghosts of leaves that fell
From bliss remembered all too well,
And now by winds of Fate are whirled
Around a dead and frozen world."

MAN'S TWO WINGS

    (Paraphrased from *De Imitatione*.)

WHEN life seems dreary,
    And thou art weary
Of earthly things —
If then thou yearnest
In holy earnest,
  For what peace brings,
Thou mayst soar to heaven
On pinions given
  To souls like thine:
    Simplicity
    And purity
    Will be for thee
Those wings divine.

In More Serious Mood

IF WE WERE TO DIE TOGETHER

IF we were to die together
    Should we wander hand in hand
Thro' the dark mysterious gateway
    To the unseen land?

Should we comfort one another
    In the strangeness of the way,
Till our eyes beheld the brightness
    Of the dawning day?

Were it so my heart would never
    Fail me at the thought of death.
Never would a pang of doubting
    Haunt my parting breath.

Life or death with thee to share it
    Gives no room for fear —
I were blest in joy or sorrow —
    Whether there or here.

THE BROKEN VOW

THE youthful monk, Aloysius,
    Knelt alone in his gloomy cell,
And scourged his quivering body
    As the shades of evening fell.
    (He heard the vesper bell.)

In More Serious Mood

A solemn vow he had taken
  To renounce all earthly love,
And to keep his heart turned ever
  To the Christ on the cross above.
      (O Spirit send thy Dove!)

But it chanced that athwart his pathway
  A beautiful woman came,
And the one sweet glance that she gave him
  Had set his heart aflame.
      (The Tempter wrought the shame!)

In spite of prayer and fasting,
  Of sackcloth and of rod,
The vision of the maiden
  Rose 'twixt him and his God.
      (Thorny the path he trod!)

He heard the solemn chanting
  Of monks in the chapel dim,
But the secret voice within him
  Is louder than their hymn.
      (His eyes with hot tears swim.)

Pater noster rang their voices;
  Salva me murmured his sighs: —
"But to rest on the maiden's bosom
  Were worth all Paradise!"
      (The inward voice replies.)

In More Serious Mood

When the monks next morn assembled,
   Aloysius was not there;
His vow to God he had broken —
   He had fled from the House of Prayer.
     (O Love, it was thy snare!)

THE HARMONY DIVINE

> Οὔποτε θνατῶν
> Τὰν Διὸς ἁρμονίαν ἀνδρῶν παρεξίασι βουλαί.

Never shall the plan of mortal man disturb the harmony of Zeus. — AISCHULOS: *Prometheus Desmotes.*

However wrangling men may war
   Or jangling discords jar and mar
God's Symphony eternal,
A law-engendered purpose runs
Throughout a universe of suns,
   Each with its song supernal.

The Harmony divine! No plan
Conceived by heart of mortal man
   Disturbs its progress splendid.
For as the hurrying years revolve
The most discordant notes dissolve
   In triumph never-ended.

In More Serious Mood

THE HEART

multa in hoc mundo sunt et haec omnia cor humanum satiare non possunt. — HUGO DE ST. VICTOR.

THE world is a kingdom of beautiful things;
    Yet possession of wealth only fosters the pride!
No lasting content it brings even to kings;
    By heaven alone is the heart satisfied.

ON A PICTURE OF SUNSET IN THE ADIRONDACKS

ON mountain summits and on clouds is glowing
    The glory of the sunset; in the valley
The waveless waters of the river dally,
And shadows darker and more deep are growing.

Hushed are the winds; the tall elms bending
    Above the glassy stream are motionless
    As if entranced at their own loveliness,
With dreamy colors in the cool depths blending.

There is no sound; the robins ceased their song
    As sunset slowly faded from the sky;
    Music and joyousness to day belong —
'T is fitting that in silence day should die.

In More Serious Mood

PEACE

In la sua voluntade è nostra pace. — PARADISO, III, 85.

PEACE? Can we find it in this world of trial,
    Where battles fierce and every form of ill
And pain and sorrow and hard self-denial
    Our checkered lives from birth to death must fill?

Peace? Peace? How sweet the word and tender!
    Its very sound should wrangling discords still!
And I might find it if I would surrender
    Myself and my will to His perfect will.

AT MIDNIGHT BY THE SEA

WE sat at midnight on the shore,
    The waves were breaking at our feet
With solemn, low, continuous roar,—
The red lights on the fishing fleet
Rocked to and fro against the sky.

We saw the mist-wreaths hurrying by,
Like loving things compelled by Fate
To seek some distant, unknown state;
The moon shone on the waters far,
And o'er the golden waste a bar

In More Serious Mood

Of shadow of deep purple lay;
The offing was a silvery gray,
From which the black-backed islands rose
Like ocean monsters in repose.

Alas, alas! no words can tell
The sadness which upon us fell;
No trick of rhyme can half express
The tearful, melancholy mood
Born of the boundless solitude.
The marbled sky seemed pitiless;
The sad waves breaking on the shore
Were moaning for the nevermore —
The awful unattainable —
As down the rocks the slow tide fell.
The mist-veil seemed to shut from sight
Some deeper mystery of the night;
The very light the white moon gave
Made shadows deeper on shore and wave.

I have seen times when inner sight
Seemed opened on the infinite,
As if the flower of God's great plan
Were slowly blossoming for man,
So that my soul began to see
Some clew unto the mystery
Of what it really means to be.

In More Serious Mood

Not so that night. The darkness drew
Like mist about my soul. I felt
That there was nothing that I knew.
My soul within me seemed to melt!
Thus by the shore we walked — we two,
As slow the mystic hour crept on
And the tide turned and the moon was gone.

THE ABBÉ'S DREAM

THE Abbé Michael dreamed one night
   That heaven was opened to his sight,
And first among the radiant throng
Which filled the streets with praise and song
He saw a man whose reckless might
   Had seamed his earthly life with wrong.

The Abbé saw not streets of gold,
Or splendid mansions manifold,
   Or sea of glass, or jewels rare,
   Or pearly gates beyond compare,
Or hosts of angels richly stoled; —
   He only saw this sinner there!

The hymns of triumph reached his ears,
But brought no solace for his tears;

In More Serious Mood

Peace from his jealous soul had flown: —
"My life is spent for God alone,"
He cried; "and yet this man appears
Among the nearest to the throne."

But ere he woke he heard a voice,
Which said unto his heart: "Rejoice!
The diamond which is full of light
Was once a coal as black as night!
Judge not the means which God employs
To make the wrong bloom into right."

THE DEATH OF AVRAHAM

HURMAZD! Almighty Lord!
A flying rumor said
That Avraham was dead: —
Drawn from the scabbard's the sword;
Loosed from the bow is the cord;
The wine from the pitcher is poured;
The casket loses its hoard.

Thus, yet not thus, from man,
When he has finished his span,
Falls neglected, despised,
The body he long has prized.

In More Serious Mood

It crumbles into dust: —
Consumed is the scabbard by rust;
The bow is broken for fire;
The pitcher is lost in the mire;
The casket is tost in the brier.

Hurmazd! Almighty Lord!
The flying rumor said
That Avraham was dead.

Hearken the Mage's word!
Solemnly spake the sage,
Bent low by thought and by age: —
I watched as Avraham's soul
Passed from his body's control.

Asks an eager fool of the wise: —
"What was its form as it fled
And joined the hosts of the dead?"

The master, unruffled, replies: —
  "Form it had none. When you said,
    Days agone, 'Lo, here is our friend,'
You thought not of mouth or of eyes,
Of hair, of color, of size, —
    So now it was at the end,
(The end of suffering, sinning,
But death is new life beginning!)

In More Serious Mood

"As the formless form of the soul
Of Avraham drew near the goal
To which thro' life he had aimed
('Zadeehah,' *the Just*, was he named),
A breeze with fragrance laden
Breathed from the robes of a maiden
Stately and gracious and fair,
Who came to welcome him there.

"She was the soul of his deeds,
   His charities, faithfulness, prayer,
     Self-sacrifice, meekness, and love:
The growth of a thousand seeds,
For all that is best in us breeds
   Greater perfection above,
But the bad destroys as it feeds,
Like canker or ruthless decay.

"Then the maiden led him away,
   As a father is led by a daughter,
Thro' pleasant asphodel meads,
   By fountains of life-giving water,
To the grove of Hurmazd the Great.

"'Well done! Thou hast won in the strife!
New joy now begins and new life,

In More Serious Mood

My son!' was the welcoming word
That the wondering Avraham heard
As he bowed in the presence of Fate."

PROPHETS

(To the Memory of John Greenleaf Whittier.)

IN every age have men been sent
   To be a nation's ornament,—
To bring the Graces down to earth,
To sing new songs of love and mirth,
To make the pictured canvas glow,
To bid full streams of music flow,
To shape dead marble into life,
To lead vast hosts from strife to strife.
The annals of the world abound
With lives which deathless fame has crowned.
But while each age, each nation claims
Its noble roll of splendid names,
Once in a century appears
The flaming torch of God-sent seers,
As comets fling their threatening blaze
Athwart the fixed stars' silvery rays.

*   *   *   *   *   *   *

When tyrannies oppress a land,
When crimes abound on every hand,

In More Serious Mood

When righteous laws in the dust are trod,
When men forget that God is God,—
Then with his whip of scorpion stings,
The prophet his stern message brings;
To pride, so soon to be brought low,
Foretells the coming of the woe;
Awakes the conscience, lulled to sleep,
With thunders snatched from Sinai's steep.
To seers like these mere beauty seems
Like forms and colors seen in dreams:
Rich houses, bright and comely dress,
The dainty fare of palaces,
The vaunted triumphs of the arts,
The traffic of the crowded marts,
Are false enticements to be spurned,
Are tinsel dross that must be burned.
And so they come in camel's hair,
With locusts for their homely fare;
And in the market-place they stand
And preach destruction to the land:
"Repent! repent!" they loudly cry,
"The judgment of the Lord is nigh!"
The heedless mob refuse to hear,
The triflers jest, the cruel jeer;
And soon the hurtling stones are flung
To still the inconvenient tongue.
"My prophets, O Jerusalem,

In More Serious Mood

Where are they? Ye have stonèd them!"
But, tho' the prophet sinks in death,
The Lord's word never perisheth.
The fated doom leaps forth at last;
And when its awful work is past,
The prophet, who its course foretold,
On whom the fathers' sins were rolled,
Is by their children's children named
As one in whom God's voice had flamed.

A LEGEND OF ST. ANTHONY

ST. ANTHONY had fasted much and prayed,—
Had spent long years in desert lands alone,
Afflicting his lean limbs with punishments
For evil thoughts that came against his will;
Forever watching for the slightest stain
That might appear upon the shining gold
Of his pure life, that at the latter day,
When he must render it unto his Lord,
He might receive his Lord's most grateful praise.

And now he was grown old and sorely bent;
His frame was feeble and his eyes were dim,
His long hair and his beard were white as wool.
And as he sat before his hermitage

In More Serious Mood

At eventide, and saw the red sun sink
Behind great masses of dark purple clouds,
Down in a sea of sand, the glad thought came
That soon his pilgrimage below would close,
Soon would his sun go down in clouds of glory.

   He raised his eyes to heaven and spoke in prayer:
"Lord, I have lived apart from sinful men;
I have not soiled my life by intercourse
With filthy pleasures which the bad world loves.
To prayer and fasting have my days been given,
My nights to penance for e'en thought of sin.
Temptations have I struggled with, oh Lord,
But never have I fallen, no, not once.
When Satan came with all-alluring wiles
I yielded not, nor have I ceased to fight
His open warfare, till at last I stand
Triumphant in my hard-earned victory.
What more remaineth now for me to do?
Am I not holy more than other men?
Am I not ripe to garner into heaven?
I pray thee let my long probation cease,
Now, Lord, I pray thee, take thy servant home."

   When he had ceased, a gentle voice replied:
"Nay, Anthony, in Alexandria,
A cobbler, Paulus, lives, who has more cause

In More Serious Mood

For boasting of his holiness than thou."
He marvelled at these words and pondered long.
The night he spent in scourging his poor flesh
Until the blood flowed down his trembling limbs.
And ere the sun rose from the ruddy east,
St. Anthony had grasped his oaken staff,
And wandering thro' the weary wastes of sand
He sought the city, Alexandria.

At length, when many days and nights were past,
Before a lowly cottage door he stood,
And gained admittance to the humble room
Where dwelt the cobbler with his family.

"I come to see a man who has more cause
To boast of holiness than Anthony;
Now show me thy good works, that I may judge,
And if convinced, though old, may learn of thee."

The cobbler, Paulus, answered in surprise:
"Nay, I have done no good works that I know;
I live contented in my poverty.
My hands I strive to keep from idleness.
I teach my children to be truly kind,
And bring them up to love their father's God.
I gather them about me when I pray.
But as for 'good works,' nay, I have done none."

In More Serious Mood

Then Anthony was sore amazed, and prayed:
"Oh Lord, expound to me this parable.
How is this cobbler holier than I,
Who have lived sinless all my ninety years,
And uncontaminated by the world?"

Then suddenly the scales fell from his eyes;
He saw how he had lived in selfishness,
How cowardly it was to leave the world
And spend his long life on himself alone.
And Paradise seemed far away from him
Who late had prayed his Lord to take him home.
His life seemed wasted, and he wept aloud.
Then had the Lord compassion on the saint,
And speedily He took him to his rest —
His aged saint, who at the end of life
Had learned the lesson of humility.

AN AUTUMN FRUIT

OUR good old dominie was fond of flowers.
It was because his life was beautiful,
I think, that nothing that had beauty failed
To touch him and to make his soul respond.
And so, because I could not do great things,
Nor bear the heat and burden of the day

In More Serious Mood

By working in the vineyard of the Lord,
On peaceful Sabbath mornings, when the dew
Still sparkled on the bending blades of grass,
And made me think of jewelled scimetars,
Wielded by fairies in Titania's court,
I cut the sweetest blossoms I could find —
Red roses, clambering up the trellised wall,
And pinks from out my little garden plot,
And bright-eyed pansies, gentians, violets,
And sometimes modest wild flowers from the wood,
Which, cool and shady, climbed the village hill.
From springtime, when the wild arbutus came
(Brave little beauty hiding 'neath the snows),
Thro' the long summer till the violets died,
And when the pine-o'ershadowed river banks
Grew purple with proud harebells, and the fields
Were thick with royal hosts of goldenrod —
Each Sunday morn I brought my offering
And laid it on the altar in the church.
And when our dear old dominie would come —
I see his white hair and his mild eyes yet —
And linger for a moment just to catch
The delicate breath of heliotrope or rose,
I saw the peaceful look of thanks to God
For sending such sweet things into the world,
And had my own exceeding great reward.
And one day, when a little child was brought

In More Serious Mood

For holy hands to consecrate to God,
She leaned out from her mother's arms and took
A single pearl-like lily from the vase —
Herself a lily blooming into life;
And then a tiny bird came with the breeze
In thro' the window, and upon my flowers
It lighted like a blessing sent from God.
But now the birds have gone to warmer climes,
And sing their matin songs on orange trees;
The goldenrod has faded from the field,
And from the boughs the chill wind shakes the leaves.
O glorious fruit of autumn — red-ripe corn,
And bending barley, heavy-headed wheat,
And russet apples, chestnuts with the burrs
Half opened by the fingers of the frost!
O glorious days of autumn, when the sun
Swims in a golden haze, and o'er the hills
The grass is slowly changing ruddy brown!
I went among the fields and thro' the woods,
And plucked a dozen ears of full-ripe corn;
I filled a basket full of forest leaves,
Glowing with all of sunset's richest hues,
And red-leaved boughs of oak, with acorn cups
And stalks of grasses with their yellow seeds,
And ferns from hollows by the brooklet's side —
And bound the wheat and heavy heads of rye,
And all the grains that bounteous autumn gives.

In More Serious Mood

And so I made an offering for the Lord,
And laid it on his altar in his church.
And when the Sabbath came, my heart was full.
How calm the river lay beneath the banks,
With grazing cows and vine-clad cottages
Reflected in the mirror of its tide!
No breeze stirred in the tree-tops; yet the leaves
Came fluttering downward one by one. The boys
Walked thro' them with the keen delight of youth
In crisp, sharp sound, and longed to run and shout.
How mournfully the bell was tolled that morn,
As if it felt the prescience of some grief!
Oh, what a prayer went winging up to God,
As if the good old man, like Moses, stood
Upon a Pisgah height, and talked with him,
And brought his people's sorrows and their joys
And laid them calmly at their Father's feet!
And then his sermon — ah, it seems to me
As if I ne'er should hear his like again!
It was his last. For ere the sun was set
The Reaper with his sickle keen had come
And garnered him as grain full ripe for God.

In More Serious Mood

THE HEROES OF CUTTYHUNK

[The British brig *Aquatic* from Cuba, bound for Boston, went ashore on the Sow and Pigs Reef off Cuttyhunk about half-past four o'clock on the afternoon of Friday, Feb. 24, 1893. The United States Life-saving Crew deemed the exploit of rescue too dangerous to attempt in the hurricane that was blowing and the high sea that was running. But a volunteer crew of six men — Captain Timothy Akin, Jr., Frederick Akin, Isaiah H. Tilton, Joseph Tilton, William Brightman, and Hiram Jackson — attempted to put out to the wreck in the Massachusetts Humane Society's life-boat. They had gone only a short distance when they were swamped, and five of the men were drowned. Their families were left in the direst poverty, and immediate steps were taken in Boston and other cities to relieve their necessities and provide for their future. Universal sympathy was aroused, and the fund quickly amounted to over fifteen thousand dollars.]

"MEN! there's a brig ashore on the reef:
Come, bear a hand for their relief!
The Life-saving Crew have turnèd back,
For the wind is fierce and the billows are black!
But we can get there, never fear!
Who of you men will volunteer?"

Thus spoke a seaman, bronzed and brave,
Ready and strong to do and save.
Five fishermen shouted their "I," "and I": —
Who of them thought or feared to die?

In More Serious Mood

They followed their leader down to the shore
To enrich the world with one gallant deed more.
Parents' and children's and loving wives'
Joy and sorrow, hung on those lives;
But tho' love for mother or wife or child
Might beckon them back from the tempest wild,
Yet still with faces set and stern,
To Humanity's task they gallantly turn.
No time for farewells: no parting word
Thro' the roar of the hurricane surf would be heard;
In silence they launch the great life-boat:
It glides down the shelving beach, is afloat!
With sturdy arms they stand to the oars
Nor heed the cold billow that over them pours.
They are off! they are off! thro' the threatening comb,
Strong as Fate, white-crested with foam
That hides them from sight, that blinds them, that strives
To swallow up their puny lives!
Again they rise, they conquer; the skill
Of man with the aid of his dormant will
Master the frenzied seas which roar
With baffled rage on the ice-bound shore.
Again and again they rise, they sink
In green-black hollows which seem to shrink
Under the mass of the toppling wave
That covers the yawning of the grave!

In More Serious Mood

And the wind adds his fury to ocean's might.
Great God! how it shrieks in its swooping flight!
Against such allies man's strength is vain:
With their utmost force no inch they gain.
Up, up they mount; the crested wall
Of solid green once more may fall
And still they live; see! see! they bend
With strokes of iron; must they spend
Their manhood's might and still not save
Those nameless strangers from the grave?

One false stroke is their doom; if caught
By yonder toppling mountain, naught
Beneath the pitiless sky can help
Those hapless heroes flung like kelp
Amid the weltering waste of brine
That stretches beyond the horizon line!

There's a glare of sunset in the west,
But the howling tempest knows no rest,
And now like a horrible harpy the wind
With a sudden swoop comes from behind.
With his grasp like steel the captain is true
To instinctive swerve; the hardy crew
Make one last effort: but they are lost! —
Like a feather the life-boat is lightly tost
On the edge of that monstrous shuddering wave,
Then swallowed up in its curling cave.

In More Serious Mood

And still on the reef the wrecked brig hung,
Still the freezing crew to the rigging clung
While the doomed ship strained, while the timbers
   crackt
Beneath each breaker's cataract,
And every moment seemed their last;
But when the terrible night was past
Every man was safely landed
From the rocky sty where they had stranded.
For the sea had accepted the sacrifice:
Five gallant lives were the costly price.

Death is the portion of mortals all:
Sooner or later it must befall,
And whether it comes by sea or land
Makes little odds as the world is planned.
'T is a moment's anguish and then release!
An instant's warfare followed by peace!
But alas for those who are suddenly left:
Of father or husband or lover bereft,
With poverty staring them in the face,
With none to take the bread-winner's place.

Ah! but the world loves heroes! Now
Is the chance for the world its love to show!
"Come to the rescue! Pour your gold!
Prove that the world's heart is not cold!

In More Serious Mood

One of those men who went straight to heaven
Left seven children — a motherless seven!
Give of thy wealth that never need
Of home or bread make their young hearts bleed!"

Thus rang the appeal and the answer glowed
And the saving tide of sympathy flowed!
Now once again we have seen defeat
Crowned with victory lofty and sweet;
And tho' that boat and crew were sunk
'Neath the waves that environed Cuttyhunk,
The wreck of that vessel raised on high
A deed of worth that shall never die!

www.ingramcontent.com/pod-product-compliance
Lightning Source LLC
Chambersburg PA
CBHW030313170426
43202CB00009B/983